DISCARD

ALSO BY LOUISE GLÜCK

POETRY

Firstborn
The House on Marshland
Descending Figure
The Triumph of Achilles
Ararat
The Wild Iris
Meadowlands
Vita Nova
The Seven Ages
Averno
A Village Life
Poems 1962–2012
Faithful and Virtuous Night

NONFICTION

Proofs & Theories: Essays on Poetry

AMERICAN ORIGINALITY

AMERICAN ORIGINALITY

ESSAYS ON POETRY

LOUISE GLÜCK

FARRAR, STRAUS AND GIROUX   NEW YORK

Farrar, Straus and Giroux
18 West 18th Street, New York 10011

Owing to limitations of space, all acknowledgments for permission to reprint
previously published material appear on pages 191–194.

Library of Congress Cataloging-in-Publication Data
Names: Glück, Louise, 1943– author.
Title: American originality : essays on poetry / Louise Glück.
Description: First edition. | New York : Farrar, Straus and Giroux, 2017.
Identifiers: LCCN 2016026993 | ISBN 9780374299552 (hardback) |
    ISBN 9781466875685 (ebook)
Subjects: LCSH: American poetry—20th century—Criticism and
    interpretation. | Originality in literature. | BISAC: LITERARY
    COLLECTIONS / Essays.
Classification: LCC PS323.5 .G59 2017 | DDC 814/.54—dc23
LC record available at https://lccn.loc.gov/2016026993

Designed by Abby Kagan

www.fsgbooks.com
www.twitter.com/fsgbooks • www.facebook.com/fsgbooks

1   3   5   7   9   10   8   6   4   2

To Kathryn Davis

For their scrupulous reading and wise advice, my thanks to Wendy Lesser and James Longenbach.

For his magical cover design, my deep gratitude to Richard Siken.

CONTENTS

FOUR

ONE

AMERICAN ORIGINALITY

We are, famously, a nation of escaped convicts, younger sons, persecuted minorities, and opportunists. This fame is local and racial: white America's myth of itself. It does not, obviously, describe Native Americans and African Americans: though they are theoretically free to participate in mythic America's notions of vigor and self-creation, to do so involves sustained acts of betrayal or disloyalty toward origins they conceivably had no communal wish to escape. Oppression, for these groups, did not define the past; it replaced the past, which was transformed into a magnet for longing.

The myth elaborates itself in images and narratives of self-invention—drive and daring and gain being prized over stamina and fortitude. If the Englishman imagined himself as heir to a great tradition, the American imagined himself as the founding father. This difference resonates in political rhetoric: American aggressive might (usually called *defense*) and acquisitiveness (sometimes called *self-improvement*) as opposed, say, to the language of appeal that links Churchill to Henry V, a language that suggests the Englishman need only manifest the virtues of his tradition to prevail. These appeals were particularly powerful in times of war, the occasions on which the usually excluded lower classes were invited to participate in traditions founded on their exclusion.

Like most myths, this one has some basis in fact. There were such flights. And immigrant populations whose relocations are, in the main, escapes from incarceration, confinement, danger, or exclusion will hardly cultivate stoic endurance over initiative. The cardinal virtues of this new world depended on repudiations, the cutting of ties, and on invention and assertion. But the imperatives of self-creation cannot be expected to bind a society as effectively as does the invoking of a shared tradition. The best that can be said is that these imperatives may constitute a shared ambition or common practice; in fact, they are the opposite of coherence. Individual distinction expresses itself as distinction from the past, from the previously acknowledged limits of the possible, and, as well, from contemporaries. Still, the triumphs of self-creation require confirmation, corroboration. They postulate, at least imaginatively, a society or audience coherent enough to recognize and reward the new. The new thing makes a kind of adhesive, gluing together (provisionally) its diverse precursors in a grid or system: a fantasy or projection of common values. How this occurs, and with what restrictions, accounts for the peculiar attributes of what Americans call originality, their term of highest praise.

Original work, in our literature, must seem somehow to break trails, to found dynasties. That is, it has to be capable of replication. What we call original must serve as a model or template, binding the future into coherence and, simultaneously, though less crucially, affirming the coherence of the outstripped past. It does not so much reject tradition as project it into the future, with the self as progenitor. Originality, the imprint of the invented self, depends on the creation of repeatable effects. Meanwhile, much that is profoundly original but unlikely, for a variety of reasons, to sponsor broad imitation, gets overlooked, or called that lesser thing, *unique*—valuable, undoubtedly, but a dead end. The original is sought with famished intensity; all the brilliant banners of praise are deployed to welcome it. But to welcome it within certain limits, with formal innovation of almost any kind valued over idiosyncratic mind.

This isn't to say other gifts attract no admiration. Technical mastery continues to be applauded, though chiefly in those born elsewhere. An American Heaney would not, I think, be so promptly and passionately acknowledged. Likewise Szymborska, whose art (in translation) appears a brilliant example of inimitable intelligence. Something, whether atavistic longing or helpless recognition, keeps them, and a few others, safe here. Americans fare less well. Particularly the unique, the inimitable.

The dark side of self-creation is its underlying and abiding sense of fraud. A reciprocal terror of deficit within the self may account for the American audience's readiness to be talked down to, to be excluded, to call great art that which it does not understand. As American poets increasingly position themselves against logic and observation, the American audience (often an audience of other writers) poignantly acquiesces.

Under the brazen "I made up a self" of the American myth, the sinister sotto voce, "I am a lie." And the liar wishes to elude: to elude judgment and censure, to avoid being caught. The literary art of our time mirrors the invented man's anxiety; it also affirms it. You are a fraud, it seems to say. You don't even know how to read. And for writers, this curious incomprehension, this being ahead of the time, linked as it is to affirmation, seems superficially encouraging, as though "to understand" meant "to exhaust."

Limitless, untethered freedom has, among its costs, a kind of paranoia: the self not built from the inside, accumulating in the manner of the tree, but rather postulated or improvised, moving backward and forward at the same time—this self is curiously unstable, insecure. When imagination is immense (as in the case of genius or mania), the nagging sense of falsehood probably dissolves. When it is not, the weak place is fiercely defended.

Part of that defense is the conviction that everyone else is equally inauthentic. Or, alternatively, to locate authenticity, the truth of a historical moment, in the inscrutable. Individual, irreplaceable human voice is doubly disadvantaged. It cannot, as formal invention or trick, be imitated, perpetuated. Second, insofar as it relentlessly manifests a self, a human being neither intellectually constructed nor devised, reactive to a world dangerously like the world we inhabit, it implicitly reproaches invention's willed strategies and poses.

Central to America's myth of itself is the image of a better world, a translation of the theological vision to the pragmatic and earthly. This idea is not unique to American democracy, nor has the failure—or at least the naïveté—of its many iterations obliged a re-examination of the underlying premise. In our period, these various stabs at a better world share a set of promises to the individual, whose life is to be relieved of oppression. The idea of individual independence—the possibility held out that anyone can rise to prominence or wealth or glory—this dream of individual distinction has become a defining attribute of democracy. It seems sometimes that as democracy appears more flawed, this promise of an unprecedented self grows more fervent, more necessary.

But the self-made man, like any figure of power, depends on broad accord; his peers must acquiesce to his accomplishment. In a period in which the future has come to seem a hopeful theory rather than a certain fact, this stake in the present has intensified. The qualities we continue to prize, immediacy and scale, must be manifest immediately. Critical hyperbole confirms this pressure; it does not create it. Our culture and our period combine to support the American archetype: the artist must look like a renegade and at the same time produce, whether by accident or design, an aesthetic commodity, a set of gestures instantly apprehended as new and also capable of replication.

The cost of this pressure has been immense, both to the neglected (in whom it fosters a bruised independence that too easily becomes entrenched rigidity) and to the admired, like Lowell in the recent past, who sense their real discoveries diluted by immediate and often canny imitation. To tell the original from the copy becomes increasingly difficult.

Gradually, through this process, the bold new artist is revealed to have limitations. Likewise the new world persistently fails to sustain itself, and the known world reconfigures itself through a variety of cultural and historical changes. None of this has any impact on the vigor of the myth.

I think the reverse is true. Like all myths of the possible, the compensatory fantasy that one can make a new self survives not despite but because of its failures. For artists, because it appeals to imagination, it has great durability and great utility. It feeds hope: that it has failed in the past leaves room for oneself and one's genius.

2001

AMERICAN NARCISSISM

That the story of Narcissus has proposed itself as a focus of contemporary meditation owes something to its concerns and something to its nature: like much contemporary fiction, it is all psychology, no narrative. Impossible to film. As a static image, it encourages projections of the kind narrative limits or interrupts. As an image concerned with the self's engagement with the self, it falls quite naturally in line with one of our century's engrossing discoveries, psychoanalysis. Further, it adopts and extends Romanticism's attentiveness to the soul, or the inward.

The soul, here, is entirely hostage to the body. In Ovid's telling, the beautiful cold boy, whom love never moves, sees in the pond what others see, the depth of the water compensating for the superficiality of the reflection. His punishment is to suffer what has been suffered in his name: he also falls in love, his love as conscious and as doomed as Echo's. He knows what he's looking at: "Alas! I am myself the boy I see. I know it . . . I am on fire with love for my own self." He endures, until grief claims him, the knowledge of his passion's impossibility.

Still, this is for Narcissus the discovery of love, of feeling. Yet within the strict parabolic shape of the story, an end, a constriction as well as a beginning. Echo, spurned, is deprived of her body; Narcissus loses his life. Although the punishment devised by Nemesis initiates lucid apprehension, it is the sense of constriction, the dead-endedness of the myth, I have in mind in my use of terminology derived from the tale. That, not the birth of knowledge. Narcissism, in what follows, means to suggest transfixed infatuation, that overwhelmed awe that admits no secondary response.

The allure of the self, in this image, is fortified by the self's perpetual elusiveness: "Only a little water keeps us apart; my love . . . desires to be reached . . ." When Narcissus bends forward toward his image, the image manifests corresponding ardor. And the meticulousness of the correspondence illuminates the impossibility of the hunger: the self cannot be the object of its own exclusive desire. Narcissus never leaves the pool; he pines away "consumed by hidden fire."

Romanticism began as a corrective to more abstract, potentially sterile practice. Its insistence on the personal was, for the most part, eager, open, innocent. It made the soul an object of proper study. Study, but not, interestingly, narcissistic homage. The Romantic poet tended to seek release from limitation: through nature, through love, through timeless art. And the Romantic imagination, projected onto the myth of Narcissus, more naturally mirrors Echo, the pursuer, than Narcissus himself. The static, transfixed quality seems utterly lacking.

That quality has emerged in our century, a curious hybrid of Romanticism and psychiatry, a mutation cooler, with notable exceptions, than either Keats or Freud. Every period has its manners, its signatures, and, by extension, its limitations and blindness. And it is particularly difficult, from the inside, to recognize such characteristics: omnipresence makes them invisible. If they are noticed at all, they are taken as marks of progress; the limitations we have been trained to see as limitations are no longer evident.

Contemporary literature is, to a marked degree, a literature of the self examining its responses. Focus varies; likewise (obviously) talent. The focus can be political (as in Forché's best work), or moral/psychological, as memorably practiced by Bidart and McMichael. Or it can be aesthetic, as in the work of Strand. These categories are not pure: they are introduced to sketch in a territory. And similar examples exist in prose, beginning with James's elaborate scrutinies. The self, in this sense, was the nineteenth century's discovery, an object, for a time, of rich curiosity, its structure, its responses, endlessly absorbing. And as long as it was watched in this spirit of curiosity and openness, it functioned as an other; the art arising from such openness is an art of inquiry, not conclusion, dynamic rather than static.

Narcissistic practice, no matter what ruse it appropriates, no matter what ostensible subject, *is* static, in that its position vis-à-vis the self is fixed: it expects, moreover, that the world will enter into its obsession. A first, an easy assumption would be that such practice derives, in the United States certainly, from Whitman's exhibitionism and bravura.

I think otherwise. Whitman's gesture, the exemplary self, differs profoundly from the insular, superior self posited by Narcissus. Like a child playing "Simon Says," Whitman demands to be followed. Or replicated, a brilliant compensation (possibly) for procreative limitation. Underlying narcissism is a tacit hierarchy: the only visible other is the self. Whereas the sweep of Whitman's categories and generalizations (like the casting call of an epic director: seven beautiful men, four pregnant women), while hardly convincing as portraiture, in its democratic stubbornness dissolves hierarchy. The marvel of Whitman is his inspired conviction regarding the elasticity of the form—his sense of what a line could be, what a poem could be. The lines themselves, their very shapes and sounds, their intent to include (think how they resist enjambment) are at odds with narcissism's restricted gaze. Narcissus's plight arises from his disdain for others, for those whose love he neither returned nor honored. His fate is punishment, not accident: Nemesis's deft response. And whether or not Whitman moves us, it is hard to make a case for such disdain: he never contrasts his own responses to the responses of others; in a fundamental sense, he never cultivates the reader's addictions to his interventions. What he celebrates in himself is what is average, common (and in all likelihood he was amazed at such characteristics, as the eccentric is always amazed to discover himself like others in some respect, or as the hypochondriac marvels at his body's simulation of normal healthy response).

Nor do the two qualities that correspond, in our art, to Narcissus's beauty have any place in Whitman's work. Contemporary art prizes the fastidious aesthetic response; it also places high value on the exposure of the secret. And in the latter sense it has, I believe, an antecedent or stimulus not in Whitman but in Dickinson, though she is, herself, never guilty of narcissism's superficiality and self-aggrandizement. Her periodic hermetic coyness is like a spinster's sad stab at grooming: an attempt to attract love. But Dickinson introduces a type of veiled disclosure that will found whole schools of poetry, disclosure so charged, so encoded, so intent on limited selective revelation as to privilege the reader. Dickinson isn't narcissistic because the other postulated by the poems cannot, in its function, become an aspect of the self, though this is exactly, I believe, what happens later.

It is important, here, to distinguish between narcissism and exhibitionism. When narcissistic reverie converts to public form (as in literature), something like exhibitionism results. Like, but not an exact copy of. Literary narcissism, in its exclusive ardor, often suggests obliviousness: it sees no particular difference between private reverie and public display, so devoid of independent reality is the world. The world, it is assumed, will duplicate the narcissist's fascination with himself, since what else could possibly be of equal interest? In the sense of this opacity, narcissism is inviolable. Whereas exhibition solicits interest, narcissism presumes it. (In the soliciting of interest, the exhibitionist is capable of being wounded, which is to say, changed.)

If Dickinson does not, for all her secrecies, take secret pleasure in the production of her intensities, if her need for confidence, her unvarying need to be heard, make it impossible for her to preempt the role of the other, the obvious questions remain as to the origins of these habits, the model for the poetry that prizes its own perception. Narcissism, as a literary gesture, cannot be utterly new. But it does seem that the unmemorable work of other periods was bad in other ways: wooden, sententious, sentimental. The eye was not, I think, quite so explicitly trained on the self. This is not to say the cure for narcissism is the outward gaze. Social agenda, concerns outside the specific self, are not in themselves protection: one of the more appalling forms of narcissism is the appropriation of or annexing of a *real* other (as opposed to preempting the role of the hypothetical other or confidante). Whole nations, whole torn civilizations turn out to be waiting to be given voice: what occurs, in such work, isn't the poet seeing the world but rather the poet projecting himself outward so that he returns to us on the page, in costume and in multiple.

If it is difficult to say when exactly the habits that evolve into narcissism began, it is surprisingly easy to say when they begin to seem rife. By the mid-seventies, poets looking inward have begun, simultaneously, to watch themselves looking inward; the poet splits, regularly, into two figures (though not, as in true detachment, two perspectives); the dominant pronoun, the pronoun guaranteed to confer stylish distance, is no longer the intimate, collusive first person of, say, Eliot, or the tightrope-walking first person of Plath; the dominant pronoun is "you," the elegant everyman of the French "*on*," perhaps, but refocused. Mark Strand made this move his signature (though he had, from the beginning, defenses against what came to be its dangers). What begins to characterize American poetry around this period is a voyeuristic relation to the self. If our present taste for the divulging of the carefully guarded secret can be traced to Dickinson, our equally common preoccupation with the perceptive self, our taste for the pronoun that encourages or supports such preoccupation, is rooted in other literatures, in Rilke's tendency to elegize the present, for example, to infuse the moment with all the characteristics of remote time. And the figure of the speaker, viewed through this lens, separates from the voice of the poet. Perhaps Rilke is ill-served by his translations; nevertheless, most of the American poets profoundly influenced by his art read him in translation. And the influence does not vary, though the translations do.

Rilke's impact, which shows no sign of abating, owes in part to the confluence, in his work, of what would be major aesthetic preoccupations. With the possible exception of religious poetry, which treats the "I" as an abyss, a hunger, by turns patient and insatiable, but always waiting, always dependent, Rilke's was the first significant body of work to elaborate an aesthetic that would come to be called female. In place of the will or appetite imposing itself on the world, or (as in Keats) the soul seeking, Rilke postulated a void, an absence into which the world flooded. The self was entirely reactive, so intensely so as to be exhausted by what, to a less scrupulous sensibility, would hardly be noticed. Out of such helpless receptivity, such contempt for the initiating will, he carved a kind of poem, a kind of *pacing* utterly unique—a pacing that simulates, in its sudden stops and starts, the irregular rhythms of outside stimuli, a tree, a sunset, a human face, washing against, assaulting the soul. These poems seemed the opposite of sonnets even when they were sonnets, in that they ended open, their vastness the vastness of limitless vacancy. And yet, interestingly, the human world (insofar as it is represented as being in conflict with the self, or other than the self) is largely absent. For the world, we have memories, ghosts, signs, in which the poet sees a past or imminent self. The selflessness, the receptivity, which are, formally, the inventions of this art, are, if one reads closely, slightly tainted by an overriding impression of the autocratic or controlling. The poet lets in what allows his projections, or cannot impede them, but he calls this *other*.

No matter whose English version I read, I cannot rid myself of the impression, in "Requiem," that this is neither a meditation on a specific human life nor a poem of mourning: I keep thinking it suits Rilke exactly that Paula Becker died; dead she is his creature, a mirror of, or adjunct of, the self. (By way of comparison, think of W. C. Williams's English grandmother, all vigorous distinctness, a being plainly not the poet nor, for that matter, implicit in the reader.) Rilke doesn't mean to be looking outward in this way. The present, with its huge cast of living creatures, was of limited use to his art. His subject was longing, his natural tone lament: he required those separations that precede or guarantee longing. And part of his genius was his perception of the way we transform what is at hand into something sufficiently remote, immaterial, to be re-created as the focus of longing. That the world is transient suffices; the present, treated in this manner, immediately becomes the past and the living other is, to a striking degree, erased in being memorialized.

When the poet says, in Stephen Mitchell's translation, "if you are still here with me," I cannot help but feel that Paula Becker is far more eagerly admitted into the poet's soul dead than she would have been alive: alive she was volatile, unreliable, separate in her will. Nor am I persuaded by "in this one man I accuse: all men," by the ready identification of the poet with the woman now conveniently absent. It is too easy to identify with what cannot, in behavior, repudiate identification. And when Rilke, in the famous lines, urges, "we need, in love, to practice only this: / letting each other go. For holding on / comes easily; we do not need to learn it," I cannot help but believe that, for Rilke, letting go was in fact remarkably easy, that holding on, whatever might force engagement with the unmanageable other, was alien. Rilke tends to reserve his most passionate admiration for two states: death and childhood, in each case a mirror, an icon of purity, a blankness onto which the self can be projected. To the extent that self is formed in opposition to the world, the self disappears. The seduction of this poetry is in part that nothing is not the self. If Rilke's aim is to divest himself of the earthly, the temporal, the aim of this desire is not, as in Eliot, union with a higher other (Eliot craves the immutable but there is in his work none of Rilke's hungering after either death or childish innocence): the aim, in Rilke, seems to be reunion with a deeper self, and Rilke's astonishing images (which survive in English, in all translations I have ever read) and his hypnotic music both offer metaphors for this reunion. Great art. But art in which the seeds of far more superficial reunions are visible. For me, Rilke is at his greatest in short forms that contain his rhapsodic yearnings; the longer poems, like "Requiem," always seem oddly masturbatory, the poet constantly fanning himself into exaltations and excitements.

Rilke's other major insight was the extent to which the present could be treated as a subject for elegy. The future had begun to disappear, and would continue—terrifyingly—to do so. The old postulates and images, both heaven and the ongoing physical earth, were giving way: erosion made a natural metaphor. Rilke saw, among other things, the ways in which erosion touched even the present, in that all figures for continuity and trajectory began to seem false. Looked at in the absence of a future, the present began to unravel. Rilke's vocation for mourning (as a tonal gesture rather than as immediate human response) instinctively maps out a spiritual terrain never before visible or audible, never before necessary. He made an art that placed the self, actually or emblematically, at the center of lost time (the moment, the instant, just past); once the self is convincingly lost—as, by definition, it is in a present so elegized—it becomes the beloved. Airbrushed, a creation of the poet's will.

Are there, objectively (if such a term is possible), benign and dangerous influences? If there are, I believe that good influences, or wholesome influences, generate variety and energy. Rilke's genius, echoing in other minds, degenerates rapidly into mannerism, rue like Spanish moss hung over the landscape. His genius was tone: in the absence of what must be (since it survives in translation) lexical and tonal brilliance (matched, curiously, in English most closely by Dickinson), his luminous meditations become solipsistic hymns of preening disappointment. Whereas the poetry stimulated by Williams retains, even when conspicuously lesser, interest and substance.

We cannot choose our influences: these are rooted in those responses we cannot (and would not wish to) control. But we can recognize the grip of unproductive influence as we recognize dangerous seductions. And we can study those strategies that seem to discourage entrapment, specifically (in regard to narcissism) modesty, detachment, and humor.

It isn't difficult to conceive of modesty as a check on narcissism. The poet represents his concerns as local, domestic, filled with the noises and distractions of actual life. The key is that these concerns are not immediately transformed into metaphors for large spiritual (or political) matters. Nor are they pretexts for philosophical meditations. When the occasion is a ruse or pretext, we know it instantly: we feel, instantly, the poet's true agenda. The ostensible occasion is, therefore, doubly slighted, subordinated to what is held to be of larger import. Modesty is not the dutiful mention of the daily. If transformations of its plainspoken materials occur, they occur so subtly, so impermanently, we cannot be sure what has transpired. And, as a rule, they don't occur at the poem's end. The problem with true modesty is that it may remain forever in the realm of anecdote. If Jane Kenyon's lesser poems suffer in this way, the body of her work provides rare examples of something else: steady interaction with the literal seems, to Kenyon, the source of insight. But insight does not permanently transfigure earth. The earth, and the poet, stay stubbornly accurate, still in the process of being formed. The speaker isn't looking for reflection but for wisdom, which reposes in the outward. Because the world is never transformed, and because it consistently prompts vision, we are persuaded of both its reality and its necessity.

Kenyon's passivity may derive from Rilke; her permeability, which is more genuine, does not. Rilke claims for himself the attributes of non-being, space flooded by impressions (hence the identification with the female). But in fact he monitors quite assiduously what floods in. Kenyon is less dramatic, not the site of a flood. Her world is small, anyone's world: a dog, a garden. Friends coming and going, neighbors. And her husband, the events of life. Nor do the poems ever culminate in that tiresome *Now I see* of transfigured experience. If the dog and the garden are not changed permanently by perception, to what end, for what reason, are they watched so carefully? They are watched, I think, because for Kenyon they are all potentially teachers. Her modesty is the modesty of the good student, who sees how shortsighted it would be to cut herself off from resources. There is nothing here of the cloying sycophant. In this system, everything teaches, but not everyone is capable of learning.

Modesty checks narcissism by deflecting attention from the self. It has a native suspicion of the apocalyptic, a distaste for both the podium and the stage, all of which dispose it (tonally and literally) to the matter-of-fact. Detachment and humor operate in another way: though different in their advantages and effects, each works because each implicitly posits alternative, or conflicting, views.

Detachment splits the speaker from the self that acts in the world. Nor is self simply multiplied; the separation prompts debate. The acting self here is Everyman in the Darwinian sense: perverse, intent on domination or control. Or, alternatively, ruled by atavistic need. Detachment, by divorcing this self from the meditative speaker, diminishes the identification on which narcissism depends. That odd person doing those incomprehensible things is hardly the lucid person who speaks. I am thinking of C. K. Williams's dazzling anatomies of jealousy. They are utterly remote from narcissism's stupor not simply because they refuse self-love but because they refuse all fixed attitudes toward the self (systematic self-hatred is a familiar pole of narcissistic absorption). In Williams's art, truth and beauty are displaced by a hunger to contain as many alternatives as possible. Opposites are not reconciled; the point is to entertain them simultaneously and, in so doing, comprehend increasingly complex realities. And the poems have more other hands than a Hindu god. It may be possible to say that for Williams it is not enough to be possessed—one must also be interested. Narcissus at the pond saw self-evident and sufficient fact: an image that stopped (or started) even *his* undeveloped heart. When tears blurred the image, he felt the terror of loss. The static has no place in Williams, nor does detachment permit narcissistic bonding. The self is too guileful, too contradictory, too mobile, to produce stable reflection.

Curiously, these contemporary methods of retaining focus on the self, or on the soul, while protecting against the dead-endedness of narcissism, often occur in pairs or trios—modesty does not obviate humor, nor does detachment. Mark Strand's ironies, evident from the first, seem a species of detachment, but what has reliably checked his early taste for the static has been his developing humor. Meanwhile, imitations of his early work have swelled the archives of the narcissistic, imitations that manage to duplicate (to some extent) the wry, languid poses while entirely missing the poems' intellectual subtlety. Strand seemed, on the surface, a breeze to copy: he has always played with poses (taunting the reader faintly), always sounded, as he chose, the limpid and stately chords of rue. But as his work has evolved, the humor incipient in the early poems (which imitation, in its zeal to simulate manner, largely overlooked) has developed into a wildly supple instrument. Who would have thought "wild" in connection with Strand? And yet, the sections of *Dark Harbor* turn on a dime, the ravishing/ecstatic displaced by the laugh-out-loud funny. Strand's malicious tenderness is apparent in the early poetry, but so too are other dispositions. This is not to say he has turned himself into a comedian. The development of what is flexible in his work, as opposed to the reiterating of the stationary beautiful, has allowed him a range the early poems didn't predict.

He was, in the beginning, the quintessential poet of Rilkean lost time: always, tonally, his work suggested the regret of late middle age. In actual middle age, he has discovered a range of notes memorably wider.

Like detachment, humor divides perception. But detachment is entirely preoccupied with the self, bent on understanding the self: it recognizes that the outside world is perceived through a lens; its aim is to understand, as fully as possible, the manner in which a specific lens distorts; it wishes, likewise, to see the ways in which such distortion has impact on the world. The temperament of humor seems to me less specifically inquiring, more social (or worldly) than scientific. The split it presumes is the division between the self that feels and the world that interprets: it recognizes, in all transactions, the gap between individual sensation and appearance; it sees, for example, that its genuine suffering may look, from the outside, trivial. In its ability to postulate an outside, a reality larger than but not eclipsing the self, it generates vast tonal possibilities and, ideally, sophistication of insight. Its danger lies in its tendency to treat the no-longer-pivotal self as a static, marginal construct: it can, in heavy hands, by deliberately impoverishing the self, create worlds as stationary as Rilke's. The great humorists never fail to see, and sympathize with, the soul's longings and confusions: for humor to work as a great instrument, the earnest soul must adequately balance the easier-to-imitate appearance of its foolishness.

Narcissus staring into the water is paralyzed by passion and regret; like Rilke, he loves and mourns simultaneously. He is trying to love a temporal image as one would love an eternal image. Because he cannot move, he explores fairly quickly all the ramifications of his situation; he reaches the end of insight. Which has never stopped writers from writing.

Nor, in a way, should it. Henry James was among the first to note, and dramatize, the relation between American independence and American narrowness. It is a great inheritance, that independence: the presumption, the energy, the stubborn self-sufficiency—these are all tools any artist will need, over time. But the vanity that attends these gifts, the sense that no one else is necessary, that the self is of limitless interest, makes American writers particularly prone to any version of the narcissistic. Our journals are full of these poems, poems in which secrets are disclosed with athletic avidity, and now, more regularly, poems of ravishing perception, poems at once formulaic and incoherent: formulaic because all world event directly sponsors a net of associations and memories, in which the poet's learning and humanity are offered up like prize essays in grade school; and incoherent because, though the poems go on at great length, the overall impression is that there is no plausible self generating them. This is not to argue that all poems must accumulate into a self-portrait, or an account of an emotional state. The problem of this art is that it lacks meaning, vision, direction. Which is to say, lacking self, it lacks context. And in the absence of context, fragments, no matter how independently beautiful, grow rapidly tedious: they do not automatically constitute an insight regarding the arbitrary.

The effect of such poems is that they disappear or evaporate, like the famous effect (benefit, in some sense) of a Japanese dinner. Except it is no benefit for the poem to disappear. A strange hopefulness communicates itself in this work, born of a profound despair, the hope that, in another mind if not one's own, these images will indeed cohere, that a self will, in that other mind, materialize; the hope that if one has enough memories, enough responses, one exists. Rilke's voids and vacuums are, as paradigms, seductive and misleading: always an agenda underlies them. But ours is a poetry in which narcissism achieves its most terrifying definition: it is not an extension of the self but a substitute for the self, as though the lifeless mirror had somehow survived the famished boy. Everything outside the self has become the self; the longer the gesture fails, the more determined the poet becomes. The world, in such poems, is like the image Narcissus gave his heart to. "The thing you are seeing does not exist," Ovid tells him, "only turn aside and you will lose what you love."

1998

a matter of style; it was communicated in two ways, through affect and focus. A certain bearing, a certain gloomy inwardness, would do. But principally, the issue was focus: it was no good to be intelligent about the wrong (for example, the too pragmatic) matters; one had to be intelligent about intelligent matters, which is to say, one had to be visibly preoccupied with subjects already dignified; ideally, one was having thoughts already thought (so that they had made it to the trot, the answer book).

It is interesting, in a grim way, to see how brilliantly these behaviors survive into later life, how cleverly they adapt. A whole literature is being fashioned under our eyes, rather along these same lines.

Central to this art is appearance: less crucial to think than to appear to think, to be beheld thinking. Important, crucial, to be beheld. Crucial, therefore, to be actively thinking (or appearing to think) uninterruptedly, to behave, in regard to one's thought, like the actress who never leaves her house without full makeup. And thought itself is defined here along deeply conservative lines despite contradictory assertion. One has to be thinking about the great subjects of the time, which is to say the subjects whose merit and distinction and propriety are no longer open to doubt. One can appear (one is expected to appear) to be querying, to be turning around and examining the idea, but this little dance is a dance of appeasement, designed to silence any feeling that one's thinking is pat. The querying and dancing are meticulously ritualized, practiced in a defined stylistic field. To be outside that field, to turn the gaze from the determined philosophic toward, say, the comic is to be outside the essential category: the artist who thinks. This means that certain brilliantly intellectual writers are not treated as intellectual writers because they don't observe the correct forms: their poetry may be deeply learned and sophisticated, informed by quite radical rethinking of philosophical issues, but if the style of the poems is too lively, too grammatically clear, if it is not, on the surface, difficult, it does not conform to established definitions of intellectual daring.

Let me define the stipulations of such daring in the present moment.

But first, a historical fragment, a digression: early in the century, Pound, poet of the unsurpassable ear, declared war on the iamb. What followed, and indeed surrounded this act, was a period of enormous and profound linguistic discovery, not all of it directly related to Pound's imperative, but all of it in some manner a shucking of constraints, all confident authority and easy bravura, as though the past were being dared to stop this inspired future. And certain of the tastes of the present moment can be traced to what we now call the Moderns, with that ominous upper case, principally our bias toward the incomplete, a taste that seems to treat the grammatical sentence as Pound treated the iamb: a soporific, a constriction, dangerously automatic and therefore unexamined.

Let me dispose of the analogy, introduced to suggest the manner in which the present moment (so fastidiously studying itself being itself) glorifies its preferences. The grammatical sentence is not the iamb. The latter, as a fixed rhythmic unit, is not elastic: one iamb more closely resembles another iamb than does one sentence resemble all other sentences. Iambic pentameter can be hummed (poets often hear rhythmic structures before they hear words); a stanza of sentences can't be, or can't be before it exists. The sentence deploys emphasis to create readings complementary to, or at variance with, the logical. It works magically, electrically; its reaches, in combination with the ways in which, and points at which, the line breaks create profound dramas: all by itself, the sentence is the Bible and the Talmudic commentary. If the sentence is to be forfeited, incompleteness must be able to match, or augment, its resources, must infuse the poem (or fiction) with equivalent depth and variety. And the same demand must be answered by related tactics: non sequitur, for example.

The gesture, the protest aren't in themselves dangerous. Merely: their fertility has been miscalculated.

Contemporary poetry affords two main types of incomplete sentences: the aborted whole and the sentence with gaps. In each case, the nonexistent, the unspoken, becomes a focus; ideally, a whirling concentration of questions. A kind of scale (in the realm of intention) is suggested: language has faltered (language, which has done so well for so many centuries), overwhelmed by the poet's urgencies or by the magnitude of the subject or by the impossible and unprecedented complexity of the present moment. What's curious is how quickly this gesture turns rote, how little (apparently) there is to explore here. Certainly, on the level of grammar, the strategies of incompleteness seem to be limited: repetition, accumulation, invocation of the void through ellipsis, dash, etc. The problem is that though the void is great the effect of its being invoked is narrow. So the ambience of incompleteness becomes (after the first rush) peculiarly static. The charged moment is always charged in the same way: hovering, tentative, incipient. For variety, the poet must depend exclusively on duration. The uniquely extended dense fragments toward which this aesthetic tends begin to seem like swimmers competing to see how long they can stay underwater without breathing: unlike, say, high diving, this makes dull watching.

A more just comparison might be the bel canto line. More just and, philosophically, more accurate: how long can one linger in, elaborate, the moment, as though the length of the sojourn had direct relation to the depth of the exploration. Which is not, in fact, true. Great bel canto comments, through embellishments and elaboration, on musical structure; seductive and powerful poetry has been written along the lines I'm describing. But so has a quite terrifying rush of very bad, and very self-congratulatory, poetry. Too often the gesture becomes, like the swimmers underwater, a breathing trick; the *idea* behind it never develops. Its failure to do so suggests the extent to which such gestures are willed or constructed, despite the regularity with which this art suggests a psychological, as well as epistemological, imperative.

The dilemma can be put another way. The sentence suggests variety through its concreteness, its presentness, through meaning (or being); it initiates and organizes fields of associations which (in the manner of the void) may continue to circulate indefinitely, notwithstanding the sentence's definite (and presumably inert) closure. In the fragment, on the other hand, variety is suggested through non-being, through unspecified (because not articulate) meaning, or through deliberate non-meaning. The paradox is that the named generates far more complex and powerful associations than does the unnamed.

The unfinished alludes to the infinite, which it refuses to abridge or describe. It can hardly afford to do either: the infinite no longer answers to that term if it acquires limits or characteristics. The absence of both, the sense of the perpetually becoming, is conceived as a source of energy, also a fit subject for intellectual speculation. The problem is that there is nothing to say once the subject has been raised. Variety rests in the means by which the infinite (or the void, the vacuum) is summoned and the intensity with which its presence is recognized. The void itself, the tremulous incipience of the ellipsis notwithstanding, has a strangely burgher-like stolidity.

Non sequitur seems to me a more complicated maneuver. Or, more precisely, more various. Whereas the abyss of the unwritten, however conceptually alluring, seems oddly shallow, and ultimately simplifying, reductive, non sequitur in many of its forms complicates. It is lively, volatile, skirmishing, suggesting (at its best) simultaneity or multiplicity, loosing a flurry of questions. It is a system of tangents, not the open cornucopia of the *ah*. In its variousness, it seems earthly, whereas the lacuna is recalcitrantly soulful, alternating predictably between the intended-profound and the intended–elevated.

These unlike strategies do, sometimes, coexist (though not with marked frequency, as far as I can tell). More likely, they reflect differing temperaments, and their common basis in, dislike for, or discontent with completion may be misleading.

Non sequitur has, I think, two primary (and quite different) uses. The first, to which I will return, is true non-relation; the second, more dramatic or psychological use makes of non sequitur a code, and of the poem a diagram of systematic evasion. The mind skids from one thing to the next, anecdote to epiphany, with no visible or logical thread connecting its movement. The task of the reader, in poems of this sort, resembles the task of the psychoanalyst: listen closely enough to narrate the gaps, the unsaid, the center around which the said whirls, from and to which it departs and returns. The said, in this usage, is a shield; as the poem develops, the reader begins to piece together the deleted material: to the degree that the evasions and digressions compel in their resourcefulness (to the degree that the mind generating them interests us), the unsaid intensifies and quivers. And—the essential point—becomes increasingly specific. As in a murder inquiry: more and more possible subjects are ruled out. In this movement from the general to the implied specific, dramatic non sequitur differs markedly from the void and its invocations. The difficulty is duration: How long can we pay attention to non sequitur, attention focused enough to break the code? That there needs to be duration is plain: pattern is at the heart of the tactic and pattern isn't established in two lines.

Implicit in this poetry is the role of the other, the concept (however intentionally distorted) of dialogue, or at least response. The mind of the speaker is far too purposeful to seem playful or darting (in the manner, say, of O'Hara); rather, it ricochets, glancing off particulars, touching on them and veering wildly away, alternating between excitement (frenzy) and anxiety (or sense of peril). The poems often move as though their speakers were being pursued. As indeed they are, with the reader playing the role of the pursuer. The intensity of this sort of art arises from the conflicted desires it manifests: the speaker here wants not to be caught; at the same time, he wants to be stopped. Or, to put it another way, wishes simultaneously to flee and to be apprehended (in both senses).

Always an other is present or implicated: a force, a danger; sometimes, too, a hope of rescue.

Not all non sequitur is this sort of diagram. To treat a poem of calculated non-relation as though it were a code is to sentimentalize it. Sentimentalize because, in poems of this second type, the only binding rationale one can devise is so vague, so inclusive, so elastic as to be banal. That this is the case intends to direct reading away from such psychological probing (since it inevitably makes the poem more superficial, not deeper). Non sequitur is not, in these poems, burning revelation begging to be understood. Nor is it a private system of logic.

What, then, is it? Deep objection to the templates, the pattern-making impulses, the glib correspondences. I think non sequitur, in this use, has two major sources: delight in mobility and profound intellectual contempt for easy emotion (one might speculate that, in this branch of the aesthetic, emotion is by definition easy). I spoke earlier of O'Hara: his poems seem to me to belong to that group founded on delight. The poems have the liveliness of good talk; they are animated by the wish to be diverted, amused; their abundance reflects O'Hara's gift for, and readiness in, finding such pleasure in the world, a pleasure imitated for, offered to, the reader. This isn't simply preference for the temporal over the eternal, the momentary and fleeting over the fixed. This is, rather, an art in which the eternal has ceased to exist except as an analogue for human memory. In its place we have joy: a mind impressionable, malicious, curious, nervously and eagerly taking in unrelated bits of data. Whereas poems of psychological preoccupation assimilate (seeking in data resemblance or symbolic weight), O'Hara simply notes; he records not to infer relation but to feed on variety, the genial spaciousness of formlessness.

Ideally a poem of this type is a replica of life, but a modest replica: it makes life (of the quotidian variety) infinitely entertaining, sweetly or sadly pointless, and infinitely rich (not withstanding little patches of boredom). Because life is never called upon (for the sake of art) to make some sort of point, the reader is afforded a world utterly free of earnest moralizing, free of the elephantine heroic. And in O'Hara's work, at least, bravado and carelessness for grandeur come to seem a kind of philosophic statement, an effortless (apparently) preference for the material and present over the non-material divine (which is inevitably also the speculative). As in the talk that, to me, such art resembles and prizes, this poetry is never bland, never general, always deeply idiosyncratic: in its essence, therefore, not a leaden policy concerning the irreplaceable present moment but rather the present moment itself, unadorned, and not idealized out of its being.

But most contemporary practice seems to me to depart from this sort of pleasure, to propose alternatives for non sequitur that are neither code nor conversation; these alternatives are not in themselves necessarily problematic, but their inherent opacities and elusiveness accommodate intellectual fraud. A model for the difference might be the difference between O'Hara and Ashbery, a shifting of interest from the moment to the idea of the moment, from speech to abstraction of speech, from the dinner table to the philosopher's study (hence, from the companionable to the absorbed solitary), from the palpable to the disembodied. It can be pulled off, this gesture; its dangers, however, resemble those of the abyss. Like the abyss, it has a tendency to flatter the reader, who projects himself, by invitation, into the unintelligible, and reads in what he chooses.

The danger, I think, begins in an extension, apparently logical. What is, in O'Hara, the evanescent concreteness of present time mutates into something seemingly larger: the poet comes first to be included in that evanescence and then, easily, to be the center of it.

As this aesthetic has developed, philosophical profundity (or what stands on the page as proof of it) is that which is most removed from the psychological, that realm in which the plight of self, of individual human consciousness, is most explicit. Fueling this move away from the psychological is an inescapable awareness, the awareness that drives much of our art, and has for some time: the self is limited, a construct, not a fate. But it does not follow that to excise the self is to annex limitlessness. In its most common manifestations (those most remote from the poles represented by Eliot and O'Hara), non sequitur resembles the strategies of grammatical omission in its prizing of the nonexistent (in this case, tone or point of view), its complacent notion that, if the highest art is without agenda, the shortest route to it is the eradication of sustained individuality, that hotbed of agenda, as it might be revealed through language-as-voice, language saturated in self.

Mind, in these poems, systematically refuses to impose or infer meaning. An admirable and promising intention with a curious result: the *action* of refusing meaning (i.e., the substance or body of the poem) is unvaried, regardless of particulars.

It is eerie to watch this art develop; to see, on one hand, its immense security as to its scale and groundbreaking importance, and, on the other, the dazzling ease of its fabrication, once the principal tropes are in place. And to see the rigorously incoherent claim for itself the stature of thought.

We have made of the infinite a topic. But there isn't, it turns out, much to say about it. Which leaves only the style of the saying. A fact that makes the strategies under discussion, these attempts to enlarge the poem's formal and ideological scope, oddly poignant: style of saying hardly leaves behind the self.

Certainly the art of incompleteness makes that self startlingly present. The silenced abandon of the gasp or dash, the dramatized insufficiency of self, of language, the premonition of or visitation by immanence: in these homages to the void, the void's majesty is reflected in the resourcefulness and intensity with which the poet is overwhelmed.

The aspect of infinity meant to be invoked is grandeur. Whereas in advanced non sequitur, infinity is enacted as fatigue: though form is not apparent, and will never become apparent, energy does not cease. Nor does anything appear to generate it: not, certainly, the trajectories of search that inform earlier shape-riddled verse, not even any atmosphere of the unappeasable. Non sequitur, in this use, is not driven; it is the idleness of the alert brain, repose not among its options. The problem to the reader is that the experience of reading a stanza is not different from the experience of reading forty stanzas. With the result that, endless activity notwithstanding, our impression is stasis (a reaction not to energy but to repetitiousness).

What the re-created void ignores or disdains is the obvious literalness of the page, its palpability, its four sides. (Technology, I suppose, may eliminate this problem, but the disposition to ignore the obvious seems likely, then, to manifest itself in some other way: what is at issue is the prevailing of will over nature.) Thought, at the moment, rails against limits (which, in very concrete ways, it simultaneously overlooks). Limits seem somehow dull, politically aligned with fetters and chains, spiritually aligned with a too-terrestrial imagination. The poet who allies himself with the abyss intends to acquire its mystery and scope. What this loses for poetry, potentially, is genuine earthly ignorance and its attendant craving to be relieved of ignorance, salient properties of the human mind; this ignorance and this craving, when conjoined to do their utmost with the world as presented, can more persuasively allude to the void, the that-which-is-missing, and more profoundly represent the drama of human insufficiency than can most stylistic gestures.

As for endlessness versus closure: read Milton's sonnet on his blindness, with its cycle of instigating actions. The poem, you will see, never ends, only begins again: "When I consider . . ." For proof, set it in the past, changing the verbs. Then, indeed, it ends. And yet it is, as Milton wrote it, in its turning and turning, a closed form.

I came to this subject because I am, myself, drawn to the unfinished, to sentences that falter. I dislike poems that feel too complete, the seal too tight; I dislike being herded into certainty. And I have sought and admired (and tried to write) poems in which questions outnumber answers.

But this question remains: How much looseness, or omission, or non-relation, is exciting? And when do these devices become problematic, or, worse, mannered? My preference for the not-perfectly-coherent makes it particularly troubling to observe the degree to which lacunae and the improbable transitions of non sequitur have come to seem less thrilling than they used to seem. And I am somewhat more alert to the fact that, in practice, we tend to infuse these gaps with a vast range of feelings not actually suggested but rather not ruled out. Such diffuseness of response is at odds with what I want of art: helplessness, the sense of the poem as inescapable trajectory.

And yet, and yet. The fervent approbation that continues to greet poems of the sort described here reflects a sense, building in both poets and serious readers, that form is in danger of atrophy or stagnation. I mean here not simply the closed, certain forms of sonnet and sestina, but form in the largest sense, as a shape made by perception: shape conferred, sometimes, but always, ultimately, shape that makes thought visible or comprehensible. Our too-eager welcoming of the facile experimental, the derivative experimental (if that is not an oxymoron), suggests that a gulf has been widening between the world as it has been perceived in poems (mysteriously ready to yield insight) and the world as we live it. As feelings about *being* change, whether that change is willed or not, the stately and noble sounds of concluded perception, all the well-made boxes, seem in their solidity weirdly nostalgic. If Ashbery appears to be for so many readers the poet of our time, it may be because he is (as O'Hara wasn't particularly) alert to, absorbed by, the problems raised in this discrepancy, and because (unlike Eliot, who aspired to be annexed by the sublime) he is willing to disappear, to dissolve in the void—or, more accurately, to exist in particles, piecemeal: not "voice" as we know it, but strands of consciousness woven through the densely incomprehensible.

As a nation, we identify ourselves with, pride ourselves on, discovery. And so are ready, always, to anticipate, to make assumptions: to experience setting out as arrival, to mistake ceremonious announcement of entrapment for escape from entrapment, to conflate the reiteration of dilemma with creation of a new thing.

I prize (as writers are prone to prizing) instinct, guesswork, nerve. But it may be that certain forms and choices need to be reviewed more closely than others, particularly those forms in which theory and intention displace scrutiny. I think we should question these choices a bit more, in the cold dawn.

1999

ON *BUDDENBROOKS*

Buddenbrooks ends when there are no men left. Nothing ends a dynastic novel so efficiently as the end of reproduction, which means one sex has to vanish. This does not necessarily suggest that the other triumphs. In this instance, I would say not.

Who, in the last scene, is left? Gerda, with her violin and her blue-shadowed eyes, like Homeric epithets. But Gerda is going back to Amsterdam, to her father, the only man still standing. (Christian, in the institution, is not exactly standing.) She returns, it is understood, to music, having been on loan to the world for twenty-one years. Presumably, she will inhabit again an identity not relinquished in Germany but not fully lived. Her German years appear to have marked her not at all. The degree to which this is the case is suggested by her prompt departure; with Hanno gone, nothing holds her. She is not a Buddenbrook; she was never a Buddenbrook. Present for nearly the whole of the novel, she remains substantial but shadowy, her motives opaque. Opaque, initially, to Tony, her schoolmate, later to the reader. Why does she marry Thomas? Their courtship, like Hanno's death, occurs offstage. Passion, we assume (we would marry Thomas, too). And yet the young couple, when they reappear, give no evidence of that; rather their mutual respect and understanding are re-marked. And no children are born for quite some time (in Mann, fecundity seems to correspond to animal appetite). We do not understand Gerda, I think, because the Buddenbrooks do not understand her. For the same reason, Clothilde is a cipher, though Gerda is magnetic and Clothilde is not. (To which we might add Gerda is rich and Clothilde is not.) Clothilde is gray, scrawny, and voracious.

The dominant female character is Tony. Poor girlish Tony: so much purposeless stamina. At fifty, she has hardly changed, despite "the stormy life behind her and despite her weak diges-tion." Her skin has faded somewhat; on her memorable upper lip, a few hairs have appeared. But there is not a sign of white in her coiffure. In fifty years, Tony's imagination came up with one idea: romantic love. She was taught, systematically, a second: service to family. The second more or less succeeds the first, which survives in a series of projections. Conflict, and with it the possi-bility of change, disappears early. She is animated by the wish to give herself to something (she also wishes the importance of the gift to be fully appreciated). In a late scene, she picks up her knit-ting. I remember my amazement: When had she ever learned something so useful? (Though she has, we learn early, house-keeping skills, the one ability Tony Buddenbrook will need less and less, certainly on the grand scale such gifts suggested to their owner.)

There remain the Misses Buddenbrook, whom Erica, Clothilde, and Tony mirror: they are now all artifacts together. (Erica, at thirty-one, already has as her main attribute resigna-tion.) And Sesemi Weichbrodt, to whom the last moments of the novel belong.

Musical Hanno is gone, the prodigy whose taste early outstrips that of his teacher. The blue-shadowed eyes inherited from his mother are, in Hanno, a sign of physical fragility; he is, we know early, somehow unviable. Hanno is like Tonio Kröger, one of Mann's dangerous gene mixes; when these characters survive, they usually become artists. But Tonio had his passionate southern mother, a source, we assume, of both physical durability and maternal love, whereas Hanno has remote Gerda. Not enough. And music. Which proves no match for the bleak agenda of the body.

Among the main characters, taken together, it seems only Thomas who changes, or attempts to change. He dares. He looks—imagine!—into a future different from the present. Which he tries to anticipate, for which he tries, for himself and his family, to prepare. He marries Gerda. He builds a new house. Repeatedly, in his business and social dealings, his attempt is to anticipate large shifts, the signs of which he is quick to read. How brave, how remarkable, how isolated a figure he seems. And in the end, he cannot change enough to move from one century to another.

2003

TWO

STORY TELLERS

The poet Stephen Dobyns, who is also the novelist Stephen Dobyns, once remarked with just irritation that the narrative, as a poetic strategy, is usually misread, or not taken for what in his opinion it is: a metaphor. As though when the poet couldn't think of anything interesting, he told a story.

Like Homer. Like the Bible.

Contemporary critics prefer, it appears, the static/rhapsodic, in which the translation of event to art is more literal: what is event in the world becomes, in the poem, luminous image. In fact, narrative is also transformation and re-creation, and the use of stories managed in more ways, to more ends, than one. In the old battle to determine the greater form (a subject in itself), poet critics, eschewing the story, seem, like the Puritan fathers, to eschew entertainment, as though having a good time couldn't happen in the presence of sublime art. But the impulse to use narrative informs the work of some of our best (and certainly most original) poets. Dobyns, obviously, but also, in a quite different way, Robert Pinsky.

It is a standard misfortune of poets (and artists in general) that their work continues to be read according to whatever impressions or verdicts attended its debut. In consequence Pinsky is often regarded as a poet of extensive dispassionate curiosity and wide learning, ethical by disposition, rational in bias, a maker of grids and systems, an organizer—the opposite of the fiery prophetic, the poet claimed by, overtaken by, emotion—and, in his calm, somehow disguised or withholding. Even when, as now, he is regularly and perceptively admired, he tends to be admired for his masterful interweavings of public and private, for his formal brilliance, for the extraordinary variety of his gifts (even passionately reverential notices sometimes digress with odd eagerness into Pinsky's work as a translator, his explorations of high-tech forms like computer games).

It is difficult to account exactly for the tone of this approbation. Pinsky is neither a poet of lyric compression nor a rhapsodist—the two forms to which readers habitually ascribe warmth, or intense feeling. And readers are, often, genuinely overwhelmed by the breadth of his erudition. But neither that erudition nor the poems' virtuosity completely explains the curious reticences and demurrals of even his most impassioned reviewers. It has sometimes seemed to me that he is read as though he were a cultural historian, in whose mind individual agony and enterprise are subsumed into, or emblematic of, panoramic history. Readers are, I suppose, distracted by Pinsky's considerable memory, his grasp of (and fascination with) data. But they mistake, I believe, the background for the foreground.

This problem with emphasis is in part a problem of expectation. In the ways we expect (at present) to see (or hear) the poet, Pinsky seems invisible, more the impresario than the coloratura. This preference for the heart-on-the-sleeve heart of lyric and rhapsodic poetry mistakes the performative nature of all art, mistakes performance for essence.

Moreover, there is, in Pinsky's human portraits, an even-handedness that can seem, by present standard of judgment, concealing. Unlike most of his peers, Pinsky is not especially interested in individual psychology. Like the parent of many children, determined to appear to love all equally, Pinsky seems, by this standard, either withholding or (the explanation usually settled for) not interested in such things. We have been trained to distrust apparent absence of preference. And yet the same balanced affection informs everything Whitman ever did, though his work is, obviously, more effusive in manner. Human passion, human life—these seem, projected against the historical that is taken to be Pinsky's field of vision, merely the poignant laboring of tiny figures in a Bosch painting, or the stalwart repetitious efforts of valets and elevator boys, working hard for promotion. To the absence of visible bias, we impute either coolness of heart or, alternatively, larger, less immediate aims, focuses.

None of these assumptions is correct. And yet, curiously, none of them is exactly incorrect either. Pinsky truly is interested in history; he truly is not a poet of the struggling or transported first person. What is so strange is the persistence of my impression that Pinsky is, among poets singled out for the highest praise, the poet read both most closely and most anxiously. The poet, perhaps, whose work makes most plain the limitations of the contemporary reader, even (perhaps especially) the trained reader.

For most of this century, poets have been divesting themselves of the arsenal of devices that had come to seem static or imprisoning. What remains is tone, the medium of the soul. Set aside, for the moment, the fact that very few poets are capable of evolving even a single unprecedented tone: the depressing corollary of this divestment has been marked atrophy of skills within the reader. Because Pinsky isn't using tone as an instrument of hasty self-portraiture, tone is hard to fix, fluid: for all their dazzling aural pleasure, these are not poems made to be acted out in Theater 101. Moreover, in Pinsky's art, form does what we have come to believe only tone can do. That is to say, form here is not intellectual construct but rather metaphor. For the poems to be understood at all they must be apprehended entire, as shapes.

I said earlier that readers have mistaken the background for the foreground. It may be more accurate to say that they miss the larger scrim against which history is projected, by which it is dwarfed. History, in these poems, is a means not an end: to view it as an end is to miss the awe that permeates Pinsky's work.

History is what human action accumulates into. If Pinsky is not particularly interested in psychology, he is gripped by cause and effect. Hence (at the most obvious level) the mechanical figures. Hence, formally, the larger musical analogies, the way, in poem after poem, one figure answers another figure, like jazz improvisations: birdsong, shard of narrative, shimmer of tree over water. The overwhelming preoccupation of the poems is less history than what lies beyond history: chaos, eternity. Projected against this unknowable void, history takes on the poignancy of what is (in other poets) the property of individual life. And the need to understand the shapes of history is driven by the hunger to know how chaos works: the poems try to outsmart, second-guess, human limitation: all their constructions are postulates, the single provable side of an algebraic equation, a seeking after parallel inference. Human life is to history as history is to chaos. Pinsky is less a synthesizer of data than a student of the great mysteries: against the background of the eternal, the void, stories are musical phrases, simultaneously completed formal shapes and inconclusive fragments.

Narrative elements, characteristically, figure in, but do not dominate, the poems. Even when, as in "From the Childhood of Jesus," the story gives its shape to the whole, the poem invokes, in its closure, the shifting ground of the eternal, in a classic cinematic dissolve:

> . . . The moon

> Rose higher, the Jews put out their lights and slept,
> And all was calm and as it had been, except

> In the agitated household of the scribe Annas,
> And high in the dark, where unknown even to Jesus

> The twelve new sparrows flew aimlessly through the night,
> Not blinking or resting, as if never to alight.

Precisely because stories are not explored as psychological archetypes, Pinsky is free to use them as notes, or phrases, as a painter would use a wash of violet or sepia. A suggestion, a resonance. They fade in, fade out, unravel, and their long unwinding or unraveling is part of Pinsky's intent, and characteristic of his treatment of every element in the poem: don't shut it down, play it like a kite on a very long string, let its every implication, its every nuance, elaborate itself, express itself: if shape is metaphor, dangerous to impose it prematurely. These dramas take on unforgettable form in "At Pleasure Bay":

> In the willows along the river at Pleasure Bay
> A catbird singing, never the same phrase twice.

And then, answering the catbird, a swatch of story:

> Here, under the pines a little off the road
> In 1927 the Chief of Police
> And Mrs. W. killed themselves together
> Sitting in a roadster. . . .

Layer after layer, the poem builds. The tenor in his clown costume finishing his aria, applause, cheers, other stories, all accumulate into the long trance, the held note of Pleasure Bay, our little errand in the world. The Chief and Mrs. W. come back again in the poem as they meant to, having died "to stay together, as local ghosts." No poem I can think of renders so indelibly the evanescence of the palpable:

> Here's where you might have slipped across the water
> When you were only a presence, at Pleasure Bay.

That the poem begins and ends with the same words, the first line echoed in the last line, makes it seem to have occurred in a heartbeat, or less than a heartbeat, all the stories, the war, the catbird, accumulating (in the absence of lyric compression) into the lyric moment: stopped time. Only in Pinsky's art, lyric time pulses and quivers, like the tenor's vibrato, shifting, adjusting. "At Pleasure Bay" (a title in itself rich in associative possibility) never undertakes to describe or fix the consciousness in which it occurs. Toward the poem's midpoint, "Shivers of a story that a child might hear / and half remember . . ." simulates the birth of awareness as much as it names a focus. In lesser hands, the poem would turn on itself here, the various elements reiterated, reconverging, as a mind forms itself around these details, sounds, mica chips of narrative. But as Pinsky designs the poem, the emerging "you" who dominates its latter third presides over a movement increasingly spectral, non-concrete: the fixed verbs of the story, of the catbird's song, the "killed themselves together" of historical time, become the loose hypotheses of eternal speculation, as though individual mind and individual identity were the most, not least, elastic element:

> Here's where you might have slipped across the water
> When you were only a presence, at Pleasure Bay.

We don't respond to the narrative elements in Pinsky as we respond to stories, in part because outcome isn't at issue. The materials are either the materials of legend or, more typically, the narrative comes to us in pieces or summaries; these are, with the sensual data more common to poetry, components of developing perceptive life: one brain cell imprinted with a bird call, one with an old story, their apparently arbitrary juxtaposition less arbitrary than it initially seems—we have to back away a bit, so that perspective grows wide enough to accommodate diversity.

The visual correlative of a Pinsky poem would be an arc yearning upward. A poem by Stephen Dobyns is nothing like that: where Pinsky is essentially meditative, the poems elaborating themselves in coils and spirals, Dobyns's poems are a rapid downward trajectory, the poems' accumulating mass increasing their speed. Where Pinsky is speculative, Dobyns is apocalyptic, his use of narrative material much closer to what prose reading leads us to expect. Here, typically, the story shapes the poem; like the great novelists, Dobyns has a moral vision; he seems, sometimes, a cross between Jonathan Edwards and Quentin Tarantino, with something of Twain's slyness mixed in. The poems are fierce, impatient, judgmental, wildly funny. He has not been, as Pinsky has, praised and misunderstood. Neither has he received (except from other poets, among whom he has the status of a hero) the kind of attention his gifts deserve. His practice of several arts (and his staggering productivity) unnerve readers who have adopted a mantra concerning range: it bespeaks, they think, superficiality. Like all mantras, this simplifies judgments. In any case, the manifold examples of Dobyns's mastery continue to appear with stubborn frequency under various numbers in the Dewey Decimal System. Dobyns's range has cost him attention; so has his wit. Though the poems move like slalom runs, hair-raising, relentless, they are (many of them) too entertaining, too well written (to invoke Pound's notion) for classroom pieties. No one devises wilder, more unexpected occasions. But Dobyns's brilliance lies less in his initial inventiveness than in his sustained resourcefulness: in poem after poem, that resourcefulness builds, invention doubling and tripling like poker stakes.

His habit is to begin casually:

> This morning, because the snow swirled deep
> around my house, I made oatmeal for breakfast.

The poem is "Oatmeal Deluxe." And the slight adjustments and modifications and amplifications that follow seem initially perfectly reasonable:

> At first it was runny so I added more oatmeal . . .

Within a few lines, though the radio is "playing Spanish music," the speaker has become "passionate." And a great deal of oatmeal is being generated. Characteristically in Dobyns the casual occasion gets very quickly out of hand, the figurative taken too literally; even his wittiest poems generate, in their pacing, some flicker of dread.

It matters that this poem, in which the amassed pots of oatmeal become "souvenir ashtrays" and, eventually, an erotic Galatea, begins innocently; it matters that, once begun, its momentum is unstoppable. Life, Dobyns means us to see, is all momentum, speeding up as the end approaches; it won't (like poetry) stand still.

At a certain point in the poem, under the influence of that inspiring Spanish music, the impulse toward creation dislodges the impulse toward mass production (as in the evolution of the mind or of civilization); the many pots of starchy clay become a woman made of oatmeal, and the poem reveals itself as parable, not anecdote.

One of the conclusions you come to, after studying the work of Stephen Dobyns for a few decades, is that it is possible to be inventive and obsessive simultaneously (Frank Bidart's career offers another example of this phenomenon). Dobyns understands that the obsessive writer runs the risk of self-imitation: he deals with this risk in several ways, partly by shrugging it off, knowing that in a career so monumentally fecund, larger architectural paradigms must sooner or later be apparent, and partly, crucially, through the combining of dramatic resourcefulness with a sort of tonal fearlessness. No one since Plath (and, before Plath, no one since D. H. Lawrence) has taken on the reader in such inspired and varied confrontations: this is one of poetry's genuinely thrilling tactics—impossible *not* to react (it is also, interestingly, the most dramatic way in which Dobyns *is* misunderstood, mainly by listeners who mistake the strategies of art for personal violence, personal aggression). As a tactic, combativeness of this kind must be inventive; we arm ourselves very quickly as readers;

for combativeness to work, it must surprise us, throw us off guard. Too, there must be a sense of something more serious at work than simple misanthropy. Dobyns's confrontations are rooted in, fueled by, his insistence that we recognize our own taste for palatable falsehood, and, having recognized it, recognize its capacity to destroy feeling.

The diversity of Dobyns's scenarios has a second function (beyond what it accomplishes in service of tone), a function specifically connected to the obsessive core of his work. The story he tells, over and over, is the death of hope (or delusion), the death of innocence, an aspect of which becomes, through the endless variety of the poems' locales and circumstances, its omnipresence. By showing us the wall everywhere, the poems insist that we *see* it: the hope they hold out is not the false hope of evasion but the hope that there may be, after the devastations of accuracy, durable wisdom.

As contemporary prose fiction has grown more static, evolving mainly as exploration of voice or consciousness, it has grown less explicitly moral in its preoccupations. Perhaps more clearly than any other American poet, Dobyns knows why: as an artist driven by moral passions and imperatives, he sees that only narrative can adequately represent in art the insidious onset of harm. This is hardly the lyric's forte: with its commitment to the concluded, the archetypal, the timeless, the lyric cannot hope to embody what is by definition both progressive and dramatic. Dobyns writes poems in which it is impossible to fix the turn, the moment: How do you determine, in "Oatmeal Deluxe," when, in the elaborate comic riff that constitutes the poem's first, say, two-thirds, the red flag goes up? When the speaker turns to his lover, the point is already made, the poem has proven what is now asserted as self-evident, because it has been, as metaphor, richly enacted:

>   . . . You ask me
> why I don't love you, why you can't
> live with me. What can I tell you? If I
> can make a woman out of oatmeal, my friend,
> what trouble would I make for you, a woman?

That "Oatmeal Deluxe" would not be grouped among Dobyns's harrowing poems makes the structural point more tellingly. The poem parallels creation as invention with creation as self-delusion: the woman in this poem cannot be spared suffering, but her insistence on self-delusion will prolong that suffering, and complicate it. As the turn makes plain, she insists on seeing this confrontation as a conflict of wills; the point, though, is that if she gets what she wants (a life with the speaker, the demonic creator), her suffering will begin *in* that life and culminate, after that life explodes, in a moment like the present moment, with the added bleakness of self-accusation. Why wouldn't she read the signs, why had she wasted so much time trying to effect impossible transformations? The alternative isn't freedom from pain, but the substitution of the pain that comes of facing truth for the prolonged pain of denial.

As in all the great Dobyns poems, it is possible to see, even at the level of grammar, the single fascination Dobyns shares with Pinsky, a fascination with cause and effect. (In an interesting reversal of the lyric, which freezes narrative into static archetypal configurations, Dobyns has dramatized this fascination in a book of poems based on paintings; *The Balthus Poems* construct, for the painter's riveting tableaux, dramas, story lines; they re-create the implications of stillness in a different, more volatile, contemplative mode.)

Under the poems' warnings and chastisements and ferocities, there seems to me to be a core of deep tenderness, increasingly apparent. We hear it in the turn at the end of "Oatmeal Deluxe," the direct address with its complex nuance, that phrase "my friend" (so widely copied by young poets of my generation and the generation following). Ironic, distant, and yet suffused also with helpless affection, the tribal affection of mortal for mortal, all of us flawed, doomed, embarked on courses of damaging affection, always ready to respond to Spanish music, in our foolish, desperate obsessions, all of us incipiently scarred. Dobyns's notion of the social is more immediate, more pressing than Pinsky's: he tracks damage; not surprising that among his myriad forms is the detective novel, the novel in which the self's collision with the world must, as a matter of form, involve punishable crime. But I think at bottom Dobyns means to spare and to save: the savagery of his poems is less a taunt than an intended deterrent. He is a poet appalled by human fate, appalled that what can be foreseen cannot be prevented.

My dictionary defines *moral* in a paragraph of ways, almost all of which unite the idea of character and the idea of action. In practical terms, it is difficult to separate the two; in life, character inevitably becomes behavior (though the translation is sometimes surprising and includes the various devices by which we try to avoid revealing ourselves—silence, withdrawal, and so on). Insofar as poets have been concerned with the moral they have tended to be concerned with the speaking of, and discerning of, truth; that poetry has not been preoccupied with the moral as it is transformed into and by gesture owes in part to poetry's treatment of the issue of time.

This has always been poetry's special province, a charged and resonant subject. But the terms in which time is regarded have been absolute: death, age, the loss of love. Sequential time, which enacts itself in gesture (as opposed to ritual), has no place in the world of extremes and archetypes. It has remained, though, to be reclaimed for poetry by forms more imperfect and more expansive than the lyric, forms more interested in vicissitude and ramification.

Certainly it is Pinsky's implicit subject. Time is what lies beyond history, or surrounds it—"At Pleasure Bay" makes of time an envelope, an enclosure; time, like the poem, becomes that medium in which we are suspended, curiously free of gravity (this is different from lyric suspension, in that lyric time disdains or opposes history). In "At Pleasure Bay" the reiterated phrase, reintroduced at intervals in its multiple variations, that phrase "never the same," while not *exactly* the same, stands, in the poem, for that which recurs as sound and as gesture; it stands for recurrence even as it asserts the absence of perfect duplication. And time becomes, like the physical universe, unknowable, infinite, shapely.

For Dobyns, time is all gravity, irrevocable as Milton's fall but in slow motion, with error terrifyingly diffused. In Dobyns's time, nothing can be sustained, nothing is safe: the painful duration of a Dobyns poem is a protest against the fact of time even as, in its unfolding content, the poem embodies time's effects. Dobyns shares with the lyric a sense of the inescapable terminus; unlike the lyric, his poems simulate human guile and human labor, the endlessly poignant human struggle to avoid the end.

Ultimately, no attempt to distinguish narrative from lyric can depend simply on the presence of sequential action. Set aside the obvious objections: the inherently sequential language itself, whether written or spoken, which, in following sentence one with sentence two invokes or simulates chronology, so that even stationary outcry unfolds dramatically. Consider, simply, visible or gestural action, of which there are, I think, two major types. When Apollo pursues Daphne and Daphne turns into a laurel tree, something occurs that, despite its narrative structure, seems unmistakably the terrain of lyric: the story of Daphne enacts two states, linked by a hiatus of pursuit; it moves through time not as evolutionary unfolding but toward transformation, toward a condition independent of time, one thing or one state having become another. Said another way: when Daphne attains her true or ideal form, that transformation terminates action; time freezes into paradigm. But emblem and paradigm are not the only means by which the true, or eternal, or soulful can enter poetry; they are, simply, the means by which poetry stabilizes the true. My use of the term "narrative" means to identify a habit of mind or type of art that seeks to locate in the endless unfolding of time not a still point but an underlying pattern or implication; it finds in moving time what lyric insists on stopped time to manifest. Plainly, pattern cannot be inferred from two states or gestures: if pattern sketches in the paradigmatic, it doesn't do so by resisting mutation. It is precisely such relentless mobility that occurs in the work of both Dobyns and Pinsky, in the proliferating oatmeal shapes of "Oatmeal Deluxe" and in Pinsky's unstoppable river: an unfolding, as opposed to the iconic stasis of which the laurel tree makes an example.

The glory of the lyric is that it does what life cannot do: this also means that it is less flexibly responsive to life, more defined by the poet's obsessions and associations. Over centuries, this can mean stagnation within the form, as the inventions of genius come to be incorporated as norms. Neither Pinsky nor Dobyns has the look on the page of the cutting edge, the experimental: no showy contempt for grammar, no murky lacunae, no cult of illogic. And yet it seems to me that in the richest way this is what they are: they enlarge the definition of the art.

1997

ON REALISM

It is entirely possible that I have never had an accurate sense of what is called realism in that I do not, as a reader, discriminate between it and fantasy.

My earliest reading was Greek mythology. As with my prayers, nothing was ever deleted, but categories were added. First the Oz books. Then biography, the how-to books of my childhood. How to be Madame Curie. How to be Lou Gehrig. How to be Lady Jane Grey. And then, gradually, the great prose novels in English. And so on. All these made a kind of reading different from the reading of poetry, less call to orders, more vacation.

What strikes me now is that these quite disparate works, *Middlemarch* and *The Magical Monarch of Mo*, seemed to me about equal in their unreality.

Realism is by nature historical, confined to a period. The characters dress in certain ways, they eat certain things, society thwarts them in specific ways; therefore the real (or the theoretically real) acquires in time what the fantastic has always had, an air of vast improbability. There is this variation: the overtly fantastic represents, in imagination, that which has not yet happened (this is true even when it locates itself in a mythic past, a past beyond the reach of documented history). Realistic fiction corresponds roughly to the familiar and present reality of the reader; its strangeness is the strangeness of obsolescence or irrecoverability. Regarding this obsolescence one is sometimes grateful, sometimes mournful. Though the characters in their passions and dilemmas resemble us, the world in which these passions are enacted is vanished and strange. In the degree to which we cannot inhabit that world, the formerly real becomes very like the deliberately unreal.

The fantastic exists as hypothesis and dream: if everything were different it might be different thus. Whereas the formerly real documents what cannot recur; we are fascinated by the historical record (which seems *ours*) and by the parallels.

That the moment or sequence represented by realism will never recur infuses the work with premonitions of ending. How will it end? Will they die? Will they fall in love? This shaping mechanism intensifies the sense of a discrepancy between realism and actual life. Less critical than the decisiveness of plot is the atmosphere conferred by the function of dying and falling in love. We read anticipating the end, foreseeing it, guessing it, trying to fend it off. In this regard, it is indeed realistic: the end is beyond our influence or control. The passionate, enthralled helplessness of the reader resembles the anxious helplessness of humankind. Once the end is itself submerged in time, in its impervious trajectory, we have moved from realism to philosophy.

The fantastic ends differently, since it never began, or began only once we concurred in its hypotheses. It ends provisionally, also with our cooperation. Then, perhaps, if we agree, it begins again. Perhaps with small revisions or alterations.

To the reader, these distinctions are dwarfed by immense similarities.

How did the child understand books? As an invitation to live in the head for a while. As the gift of furniture or trappings for that life. Life in the head became, for the book's duration, more focused, rich with alien detail. Whereas poetry was the way you thought when you were reading or being, independent of the finite freckled self. But that is another subject.

2004

THE CULTURE OF HEALING

In regard to the restorative power of art, a distinction must be made between the experience of the reader and the experience of the writer. For the reader, a work of art can make a kind of mantra: by giving form to devastation, the poem rescues the reader from a darkness without shape or gravity; it is an island in a free fall; it becomes his companion in grief, his rescuer, a proof that suffering can be made somehow to yield meaning.

But the relation of the poet to his composition seems to me other.

We live in a culture almost fascistic in its enforcement of optimism. Great shame attaches to the idea and spectacle of ordeal: the incentive to suppress or deny or truncate ordeal is manifested in two extremes—the cult of perfect health (both physical and psychological) and, at the other end, what could be called a pornography of scars, the seemingly endless flood of memoirs and poems and novels rooted in the assumption that the exhibition of suffering must make authentic and potent art. But if suffering is so hard, why should its expression be easy? Trauma and loss are not, in themselves, art: they are like half a metaphor. In fact, the kind of work I mean—however true its personal source— is tainted by a kind of preemptive avidity. It seems too ready to inhabit the most dramatic extremes; too ready to deny loss as continuity, as immutable fact. It proposes instead a narrative of personal triumph, a narrative filled with markers like "growth" and "healing" and "self-realization" and culminating in the soul's unqualified or comprehensive declaration of wholeness, as though loss were merely a catalyst for self-improvement. But as the power of loss is undermined or denied, so too does the speaker come to seem entirely constructed, inhuman.

My own experience of acute suffering, whether in the life or in the work, is that during such periods I do pretty much nothing but try to stay alive, the premise being that if I stay alive I will at least be present in case something changes. I have no sense of myself as trying to effect change. Nor do I believe that the peculiar resilience of the artist is a function of art's restorative power. The artist's experience of his own work alternates panic with gratitude. What is constant, what seems to me the source of resilience (or fortitude), is a capacity for intense, driven absorption. Such absorption makes a kind of intermission from the self; it derives, in the artist, from a deep belief in the importance of art (though not necessarily his own art, except in the presence of its being made). At intervals throughout his life, the artist is taken out of that life by concentration; he lives for a time in a suspension that is also a quest, a respite that is also acute tension. His belief in art, and investment in art, in the dream of articulation, project him constantly into the future—the hypothetical moment in which comprehensive darkness acquires limits and form. For nostalgia, it substitutes terror and hunger; for the ideal of restoration it substitutes an ideal of discovery. Toward which end, the artist, like the analyst, cultivates a disciplined refusal of self-deception, which is less a moral position than a pragmatic act, since the only possible advantage of suffering is that it may afford insight.

The great crime writer Ross Macdonald says that he, "like many writers," "couldn't work directly with [his] own experiences or feelings." For Macdonald, a narrator "had to be interposed, like protective lead, between [himself] and the radioactive material." For the poet, time suffices, in that it introduces an altered perspective. But those works of art that can be traced directly to specific events—however long after the fact they may be created—involve the artist in a particular relation to these events. The poem is a revenge on loss, which has been forced to yield to a new form, a thing that hadn't existed in the world before. The loss itself becomes, then, both addition and subtraction: without it, there would not have been this poem, this novel, this work in stone. And a strange sense of betrayal of the past can occur as the absolute of loss becomes ambiguous, the mutilator the benefactor. Such complex doubling of function doesn't seem to me a thing restored. And the agent of transformation, in any case, is time, which cannot be forced or rushed.

1999

THREE

TEN INTRODUCTIONS

Author's Note

Sometime in the late 1990s, Stephen Berg asked me if I might be willing to judge the APR/Honickman First Book Prize, a first-book competition overseen by The American Poetry Review, *of which Stephen was an editor; the winning manuscript would be published by Copper Canyon. I had come to trust Stephen Berg tremendously. He had persuaded me, some years before, to try writing critical prose (Wendy Lesser had been independently urging the same idea). That practice had already had valuable benefits, not the least of which was the pleasure of having, more frequently and more steadily, an ongoing project. The Honickman Prize manuscripts were to be screened by Stephen and his staff; I could see as many or as few as I liked. I agreed, on the understanding that I would see as many books as possible (ideally all), since that seemed the only way the award would reflect my judgment. And on the condition, also, that Stephen would read my introduction to be sure it contained no egregious errors.*

I could not have anticipated the sustained elation this task afforded. Cartons began to arrive. I had by this point in my life long experience of cartons, but for the first time they were a source of excitement, not objects of dread. I was reading to fall in love: panning for gold was how I saw it. I don't know how many books there were. Many. And subsequently many piles. The consider seriously pile. The maybe pile. The unlikely but not impossible pile. There were, in any case, a number of extraordinary and radically different books; the book I chose, in the end, was the one among those finalists least like me (which I thought would do the book good). The introduction, which I had feared, was thrilling to write. I felt I had discovered an immense talent; the act of describing it took on a genuine urgency, not unrelated to messianic fervor.

As is obvious from what follows, I judged (in short order) other first-book prizes. Almost immediately after the Honickman Prize, the Bakeless Prize, for which Michael Collier, who supervised the series, had devised impressive protocols. The manuscripts were void of identifying marks. No author's name. And, less obviously, no acknowledgments page. Screening was done by a group of poets chosen by the current judge. That same year, I was asked to judge the Yale Younger Poets Prize. This meant a terrifying five-year commitment. I feared the obligation to produce, year after year, a prose foreword. I feared there would be, certain years, no manuscript that excited me. But finalists, to whom I had by then begun writing detailed letters, could now be invited to resubmit their books. Many did, some several times. And profound relationships developed: with the work that I was reading over those years, and often with the authors, whom I would meet, when possible, for extended conferences. Not all of these books won the Yale prize. But many won other prizes, or found homes with eminent publishers. I stayed on as judge for three years beyond the original five, at which point it seemed time for another taste to determine so significant an honor (and for my own students to be free to submit their work).

Each of these books has its own narrative. Some few changed very little between initial acceptance and publication. But most changed strik-

ingly, through patient, obsessive, often inspired revision. In the ten years during which these introductions were written, I was being exposed to writers of surpassing originality, some of the most exciting writing in our language. It was one of the great experiences of my life.

IN THE SURGICAL THEATRE /
DANA LEVIN

Frank Bidart has remarked of the poet David Matias that he wrote as one in the grip of a story. In Matias's case, the story was AIDS, its power simultaneously destructive and generative.

The remark can be adapted to describe Dana Levin's first collection. For *story* substitute *image*: at the book's center (and reaching into all the surrounding material) is the surgical theatre, an image, like Plath's bees, metaphorically fertile, its manifold resonances revealed through Levin's extraordinary and demanding intelligence. The danger of such powerful figures is the danger of lesser imagination, imagination content with the first circle of revelation. What in such a smaller talent might have proved repetitious, banal, self-glorifying, is, here, the heart of an astonishing book.

The richness of its center derives from ambiguity: the raised scalpel—healing that looks like assault. A healing, an assault, aimed, often, at a baby, so that the hovering knives become at once an image of salvation and the first impression of a lethal world. The recurring figure has the feel, or, more accurately, the force of biography, of lived experience. But it is biography wholly transmuted into metaphor, which is to say Levin's experience (whatever it is, whether she is patient or surgeon) is life not simply lived through but thought through: the authority of the real combined with the larger evocativeness of imagination.

> Do you know if you want it? Is that jumble of spit and
>> bone
> so worth it
>> that you would go down again and be
> a body
>> raging with loss, each beat of the heart
>
> like the strike of a hammer,
>> spiking the nails in, to feel, to *feel*—
> I learned this from you, Father, all my life
>> I've felt your resign to the hurt
> of living,
>> so I came up here, to the scaffolding above
> the surgical theatre
>
>> to watch you decide.
> Can you go on with this mortal vision? . . .
>> —"IN THE SURGICAL THEATRE"

The book begins, though, in disturbing tranquility:

> The assistants lift him gently,
> gently. For a moment, the one lifting under his arms
>> is in the attitude of an artistic
> sorrow—It is
>> the Deposition, the taking down of the god.

In the stillness of death, there is activity. Less violent than the scalpels of healing, but more assured as to outcome:

> When they've gone, Debov sits watching. He imagines
> the sheath of bacteria he knows is there, incessant, biological,
> seeking a way in. They push and gather
> at every pore, but the flesh is sealed—
> His doing.
> Soaking in the vat of embalming fluid, Lenin looks restful,
> meditative, a high official in his bath
> in his dacha, far away
> from the controlled air of the mausoleum . . .
>
> —"LENIN'S BATH"

Characteristic is the massive weight of both passages, so unlike the peculiarly substanceless mass of much contemporary poetry, the mass of the reiterated indeterminate. Nor is this the inquiring, elastic capaciousness of the note-taker, the generous gatherer. Rather, this is mass as dense accrual of detail around particular ideas, ideas sufficiently magnetic or profound to allow detail to adhere in varied ways.

If the shape and manner of these poems owe something to Whitman, the temperament is less affable, its luminous, mortal, ecstatic reach closer (among Americans) to Crane. But scale here is less purely expansive, more corrective: Levin's animating fury goes back deeper into our linguistic and philosophic history— to Blake's Tyger, to the iron judgments of the Old Testament.

Her syntactical signatures are two. If syntax reveals, more deeply than any other formal element, the style of a poet's thought, then Levin's art owes most to, is closest to, these earliest masters. (Though it is also true that readers can hear only echoes of what they themselves have read.) But surely there is something of Blake in Levin's driving imperatives and urgent repeated questions, and something of the biblical in her savage moral intensity:

> oh doctor, angel, person healed,
>> do you think this is grandeur, to see myself
> as an avatar of healing,
>> to see in the sick child the fever of the world,
> and to say to the people in the distant air
>> circling and circling, like planets caught,
> the fires of their own
>> history's wreckage, Come down
> into the burning,
>> feel it,
>
> so you can not live it anymore.

—"PERSONAL HISTORY (V)"

Such questions and imperatives make up a syntax of insistence; its proliferating clauses, animated by a need to refine, to amplify, crucial perception, have nothing in common with ornament. This is the language of the prophet: Levin's art, in this book certainly, takes place in a kind of mutating day of judgment: it means to wipe a film from our eyes. It is a dare, a challenge, and, for all its considerable beauty, the opposite of the seductive. How remote this art is, in its scale and seriousness, from most of what surrounds it, from what could be called the ambitious minor, with its polished self-consciousness: on one end, the depressingly flawless small lyric, and on the other, facile amplitude, its very pointlessness promoted into philosophical exploration.

Also at odds with contemporary habit is Levin's refusal to

identify herself by gender. She writes sometimes as a woman, sometimes as a man (often simply as a human soul):

> . . . —this green
> brightness—
>   like a stage lit up in a ring of dark trees, where he has
>   come
> with a stick of birch, where he has come
>   to not have a body—

And later, in the same incandescent poem:

> He knows the names, from his brother's textbook,
> *calyx, lepidoptera, labia, clitoris,* he'd thought
>   they were beautiful,
> as he spreads the pictures down on the ground, his eyes slow
>   as a tracing finger, he's a boy,
> he will have this body,
>   what will he do now with the beautiful names.
>
>   —"THE BEAUTIFUL NAMES"

Current American literary life being what it is, a well-documented and scrutinized arena (the audience made up almost entirely of practitioners), a lit trail from the MFA programs through the multiple journals, it is rare to encounter so substantially, and for the first time, so mature a gift. Formed, complex, learned: but where was it through those nervous earlier stages, when we would normally have been watching it, speculating about it, ministering and judging?

It was an extraordinary experience for me, to discover this talent entire, in a book. Nor can excerpts give any sense of its scope, its music, the poems' tidal power:

To say, I hurt—

To say, The heavens are empty—

To say I hurt, the heavens are empty, the streets are
empty,
beer cans scatter, the click and tink of their tinny
bells—

To say there is a Dark Age grasping for light, extending
its bent
hands back to the other one, which had striven and
striven,
while this one doesn't even know
it strives—

And to say, The sirens are advancing.
And to say, It's 1999.
And to say, My gas bill is late.
And to say, There is no lover.

And to rise up to the stove and pour the water in the cup,
to watch the tea stain it,
while mercury opens his doctoring wings and hovers
at the edge of the ceiling,
to cocoon you,
to give you a stage—

—"THE WORK (IV)"

Sensuous, compassionate, violent, extravagant: what an amazing debut this is, a book of terrors and marvels.

1999

THE CLERK'S TALE /
SPENCER REECE

Chaucer's *The Clerk's Tale* tells the story of a marriage: the Marquis Walter marries the peasant girl Griselda, after exacting from her a vow of obedience which he proceeds ruthlessly to test. Griselda's radiant compliance makes of the tale a parable of virtue which, in the Judeo-Christian tradition, flourishes in conditions of powerlessness. The tale is a problem for many contemporary readers, possibly because virtue unconvincingly disarms brutality, possibly because modern thinking is not inclined to equate moral virtue with obedience and patience, preferring, as its standard, action and protest.

Spencer Reece's *The Clerk's Tale* is no more a strict retelling of Chaucer's tale than his ghazals are strict ghazals. Chaucer survives as resonance and parallel; for all its shimmering ironies, this clerk's tale unfolds with an oddly objective, stoic clarity; its yearning toward goodness and understanding of fortitude suggest, but do not paraphrase, Griselda. And it begins, like Chaucer's narrative, with the request for a vow:

Promise me you will not forget Portofino.
Promise me you will find the trompe l'oeil
on the bedroom wall at the Splendido.
The walls make a scene you cannot enter.

Perhaps then you will comprehend this longing
for permanence I often mentioned to you. . . .

—"PORTOFINO"

Reece's mastery of tone and diction, his unobtrusive wit, show themselves in the exquisite disjunction between "permanence" and "often mentioned." "Promise me you will not forget": the fundamental human plea for corroboration. In this case, the promise, given, binds the beloved to the lover, the reader to the poet. The common referent is Portofino, not the place merely, but what was felt there, what was intimated there. What sustains the beautiful is loss: as the property of memory, the beautiful is elevated to that permanence and durability experienced, in perception, as its central attribute. Memory corrects time; in Portofino, infinite space turned into a wall; the eye was fooled, the illusory taken for the real.

Reece's longing for permanence is rooted in a profound sense of the provisional nature of all human arrangements and a corresponding perception of an ideal. The scene "you cannot enter," the world denied, recurs. The same hunger for permanence disposes him to find security in ritual and repetition; when the clerk, in the title poem, tells us "Mostly I talk of rep ties and bow ties, / of full-Windsor knots and half-Windsor knots," he is not speaking in frustration. The mall is, in its way, a retreat; the fact that nothing happens here that has not happened before induces, within the clerks' brotherhood of service, a nearly monastic composure. Medieval obedience has modulated into the clerks' prescribed patter and repetitive tasks; in the mall itself "the light is bright and artificial, / yet not dissimilar to that found in a Gothic cathedral."

Its light touch and connoisseur's passion for surface notwithstanding, this is a book of deprivations and closures, each somehow graver than the external sign suggests. Expansive description is sealed off in terse sentences: houses are sold, dogs are given away. Against these cumulative finalities, the dream of permanence makes an alternative or corrective. And beauty, especially remembered beauty, which is insulated against erosion, functions in these poems like a promise: it holds the self firm in the face of crushing solitude and transience.

I say "self" (in Reece's wonderful phrase, that "brochure of needs"), but these poems are filled with acts of unforgettable portraiture and complex social observation. Spencer Reece has something of Bishop's passion for detail, her scrupulousness, something of Lowell's genius for fixing character in gesture (like Lowell, he also chooses props brilliantly); the wild, inexhaustible fertility of his comparisons is, though, without exact antecedent, except perhaps in the similes and metaphors of children, to which Reece adds unique resources of vocabulary. Nowhere are these characteristics more striking than in the three major sequences that give this collection its weight and substance. By turns harrowing, comic, poignant, each in its own manner combines detached, elaborate refinements of scrutiny with an eerily skittish mobility of focus, so that the poems both see deeply and move nervously, like an animal in panic. It is an effect I have never quite seen before, half cocktail party, half passion play. The somnambulistic, corrosive violence of "Florida Ghazals," its sense of grief beyond remedy, give to the surrounding poems an air of quiet heroism and deep suffering. The poem builds slowly, incrementally:

Consider the teenage boy again. His locked room is a diorama
  of loneliness.
He bucks his hips until his hurricanes of desire are arrested.
Then comes a deep silence.

Weather. Weather. How's the weather?
When I speak of the weather is it because I cannot speak of
  my days spent in the nuthouse?

Juan sinks into the swamp thick with processed excrement.
Nude paper ladies sink him like cement, silencing him.

The men in the gym slow down their repetitions, their biceps
  grow; they are silent in their strength.
When does silence go from being an asset to a liability?

The parallel isolations never fuse; isolation, for Reece, is plu-
ral, social. Rather, there is introduced, gradually, an event more
absolute, more devastating. What would be in another poet an
occasion for moralizing, a catalyst for change, is here merely
another horror, absorbed into the swamp.

The long poems change the scale of this art, but Reece's
breadth and precision of gaze, his often fizzy inventiveness,
are everywhere apparent, emblems of humanity and generosity.
"Everyone's a fugitive," he tells us. "Everyone." We meet many
in these pages:

There was a yacht club meeting every summer
with a cannon that went off—*baboom!*
Women arrived in their thin Talbots belts,
carrying wicker purses shaped like paint cans
with whalebone carvings fastened on top,

resembling the hardened excrement seagulls drop.
Occasionally the purses would open,
albeit reluctantly, like safe-deposit boxes.

—"CAPE COD"

Or, in the title poem:

> . . . Our hours are long. Our backs bent.
> We are more gracious than English royalty.
> We dart amongst the aisles tall as hedgerows.
> Watch us fade into the merchandise.
> How we set up and take apart mannequins
> as if we were performing autopsies.
> A naked body, without pretense, is of no use.

—"THE CLERK'S TALE"

Like Lautrec's drawings: so much *world* in so few lines!

We do not expect virtuosity as the outward form of soul-making, nor do we associate generosity and humanity with such sophistication of means, such polished intelligence. Like all genuinely new work, Spencer Reece's compels a re-evaluation of the possible. Much life has gone into the making of this art, much patient craft. And intelligence that postulates the cost of self-preservation, which is spontaneity:

> I remember the ponies in the distance.
> I remember you talked of a war, no, two wars, a failed
>   marriage—
> discreetly, without force or grandeur.
> This was before they amputated your leg, before the stroke.
> You rolled your *r*'s, spoke of Oxford,
> recalled driving in the Quaker ambulance unit in China,

where you saw an oil drum filled with severed limbs.
Pleased to have your approval, I rarely spoke.
You were like a father to me and I was grateful.
I remember the ponies behind the fence, muscular,
breathing, how they worried the grass.
The ponies said: *This day astounds us. The field is green.*
We love nothing better than space and more space.
Ah, they knew what I needed to know.
They lived in their bodies.
If the ponies wanted to kiss, they kissed.

—"PONIES"

Artless naturalness is one thing in the field and quite another on the page, where its simulation tends to produce self-congratulatory tedium. Among the triumphs of *The Clerk's Tale* is this tone, so supple, so deft, so capable of simultaneous refinements and ironies as to seem not a tone, not an effect of art, but the truth.

How are we to master suffering? Over and over, the poems in *The Clerk's Tale* discover in modesty a discipline by which the desire to affirm can overcome repeated disappointment that threatens to become withdrawal or despair. They take solace in simple decency; they admire dignity, as they admire the natural forms in which spontaneity survives. But Reece's art is not modest (as it is not sentimental or pious). By some bizarre alchemy, modesty of expectation fuels in this poet a profound capacity for wonder—at nature, at language, at human beauty and bravery, at vistas and interiors. I felt, reading this book, a sense of Herbert's luminous simplicities somehow crossed with Anne Carson's caustic epigrammatic brilliance and Merrill's perfect pitch. An odd sensation, as though the ingenious confectioner were also the postulant. I do not know a contemporary book in which poems so dazzlingly entertaining contain, tacitly, such deep sorrow.

"The frankly marvelous has not always been in disrepute," James Sledd remarks in his discussion of Chaucer's Griselda. I felt emanating from Spencer Reece's work a sense of immanence that belongs more commonly to religious passion; it is a great thing to have it again in art:

> When the ficus beyond the grillwork darkens,
> when the rind cools down on the lime,
> when we sit here a long time,
> when we feel ourselves found,
>
>   . . .
>
> we will turn at last,
> we will admire the evening's fading clues,
> uncertain of what the dark portends
> as another season ends
> and the fabulous visitors depart in luxury cars,
> we will savor the sharp light from the summer stars,
> we will rejoice in the fronds tintinnabulating down these
>   empty streets,
> these beautiful streets with all these beautiful names—
> Kings, Algoma, Via Bellaria, Clarendon, Via Vizcaya,
> Via Del Mar, El Vedado, Banyan, El Brillo, El Bravo,
>   Via Marina.

—"CHIAROSCURO"

2004

THE CUCKOO / PETER STRECKFUS

The case for nonsense is not the same as the case against meaning. It belongs, in literature, to the holy fool and cryptic sprite; in religion, to the visionary or the seer; in philosophy, to the Sphinx and the Zen master. It is animated not by an objection to meaning, which it intends and reveres, but by a refusal of the restrictive governing of meaning by will and logic. For the tools of reason, it substitutes the resources of magic; against the rigidity of the absolute, it suggests the hypnotic power of the evanescent; for narrative, it offers collage or prism; for conclusion, hypothesis.

Such art asks, inevitably, a kind of consent of the reader. Or, in Peter Streckfus's unforgettable first book, more active cooperation: what is transacted here between poet and reader has less to do with the reader's being convinced by elegant or passionate argument and more to do with seduction. And the instrument of our seduction, for once, is not charm but mesmerizing beauty:

Great Banquet in Heaven; you see,
illustrious, plentiful, a forest, and a library kept
in its understory,

        pages and pages of paper for the bureaucrat or scholar;
a woman at the edge of a field bounding on the forest,
an umbrella yellow in her right hand,
her fingernails of jade,
on her finger a worn ring of five-color gold;

                      a cuckoo
and a cowbird about their usurpations,
and (such were the animals present)
white tailed deer, the flags of their white tails
seen out over whatever water that is.

Why is there a woman and not a man? Why is there not
    a child?
    And what has this to do with heaven?
Because you are the man, a slender penis between your legs.
Of this we shall speak more later.

                          —"EVENT"

It would all fail, of course, the effect of the spell dissipate, were the universe of this art less profoundly original, less richly imagined. An atmosphere of luminous high-mindedness suffuses Streckfus's poems—high-mindedness not in any sense constricting or pedantic or puritanical. Nonsense and mystery are not substitutes for truth; they are its consorts, engaged with it in perpetual dialogue. And the realm in which such dialogue occurs lists among its attributes purity and, to some extent, unworldliness.

The actual and the fantastic, the historical and the imaginary do not so much collide as interweave; Streckfus uses realities piecemeal, his phenomenal ear alert to continuities. Like Frank Bidart, he uses, to his own ends, materials from existing sources. He shares with Bidart a feeling, too, for ritual; there, for the moment, resemblance ends. Streckfus's characteristic mode is allegory or parable; his characteristic metaphor, the journey. (Equally characteristic is his reluctance to specify, or his disinterest in, a journey's object or purpose, as though the need that there be a journey precedes any particular catalyst.) What survives of the journey is not the dramatic arc of narrative but rather archetypal form, a kind of infinite passage, neither driven nor haunted. Streckfus's odd compressed epics, like "Event," like "The Organum," seem almost tonal analyses of narrative, so eerily exact as to compel precisely as a story would, though there is no story, merely the story's shape and cadence—no one, I think, has quite discerned the template in this manner. More remarkable is how much feeling survives: one wouldn't expect heartbreak to be among the effects of such a method, but it is.

Nor would it seem the province of this voice, a term that seems curiously inadequate or inappropriate to so disembodied an instrument. Calm, floating, speaking sometimes in the manner of the ancient soul, sometimes as the initiate: it is a voice from which all turbulence has been expelled, leaving a tenderly attentive detachment. And yet it can turn, for all its uncanny remoteness, stricken, ecstatic. Nothing in contemporary poetry sounds like the ravishing end of "Event":

> Because I'd seen them so often come here
> to the most remote part of the garden and rub the centers
>
> of their bodies together beneath their changing petals,

I considered them part of my own. And they considered me
 the same

coming to me as they did on this day.
They took one of my fruit and gave it to her, and then
 taking my

branch and stripping it of all its leaves,
and stripping her garments, they beat her with my branch,

the white flesh of my fruit running through her fisted hand
 until it held only my seed.

If it is true, as the lemons say, that he is a god, then this must
be the way it is done. I saw her stiffen, from blossom to dead

 and pregnant fruit, the white flesh almost beaten away, her
body rolled to a ball.

I saw a kind of shell within her open, its contents taken by
 the wind.

 Ah, so this is how they are borne.

By positioning his speaker in a tree, Streckfus has managed
to transcribe the great mystery: a soul passes from its body into
air; the human species is carried off like a seed. The tree, I think,
wishes to learn how it is done, this being human, since it has
been the tool of a human act, an act in this case murderous. This
is a world of transformations, mutations, the physical transformed to the spiritual and back again. The fluid long poems
move in shapely scenes and lyric episodes, in puzzle pieces: ideas,

phrases, figures recur, appearing and disappearing. Streckfus's predilection for anachronism intensifies the impression—time becomes, in this poetry, a series of overlapping transparencies; we are meant, I think, to sense what might be called eternal shapes, as though, if it were possible to move back far enough from transience and change, one would see, clearly, the large recurrences.

Peter Streckfus's quiet authority is uncommon in contemporary poetry, especially uncommon in one so young. We expect, I think, other strengths: intensity, technical virtuosity. Or delicacy, the perfection of the small thing. Not this confident serene mastery, this soaring, Streckfus's strangely distant intimacy and peculiar pageantry: he lives deeply in imagination; the quotidian, the social, impinge very little. And the constructs of that imagination owe their scale to the breadth of Streckfus's sources; he seems, often, like a seer raised in the world of George Lucas.

He is not afraid of grandeur. He is willing, like the cuckoo, to appropriate; he borrows his nests. And his evasions seem purposeful and necessary, an enactment of his refusal of the confinements of sense and firm conclusion—doors do not close in this poetry, rooms are not sealed off. And yet he dignifies a reader's need for finality, for clear answers, for solid, verifiable ground. Though he will not accommodate that need, his acknowledgment of it results in solicitude, a gentle invitation to move beyond the known, the secure:

> Let me tell you a story. A woman farmer had two she-
> goats. . . .

And the story proceeds, in the leisurely fashion of a fairy tale, a bedtime story:

Springs before she'd left off milking,
she always had a few kids

                  hopping in the yard like cupids.
The billy she penned separately so the milk wouldn't taste
   like sex.
Then, death approached with the rustic

twittering of juncos, the place a shambles, the tree rats
                        deep in the brush.

I know nothing
     of goats. I apologize beforehand that they become
       tangled in
my story. The billy will wish it'd never had horns,
                   its whole life spent
licking its own penis and scratching those castles on its head
as if they were boils that needed lancing;

the she-goats will be in chains, put on a run by a well
   meaning city-man . . .

A parable, an allegory, whose title, "Why I Slept with Him,"
invites the reader to expect certain satisfactions. But for Streckfus,
that is the problem, that expectation of satisfaction, of the single
answer. To know how it felt to be the other? Because there was
no choice? Perhaps, perhaps not:

                        . . . —See? How he pulls
the black one's leg from the chain about the little

one's neck in the moon light? And how, understanding

goats as social animals, he will inevitably run them
out again the next day?

And then it is the next day; the imagination draws confidence
from accurate prediction:

> . . . Let's go down and untangle them.
> We'll take their places.
> Here he is with his well meaning hands.
> The pupils of our eyes are sliced off at the top and the bottom
> and we've lost our voices. Have you ever seen how sad
> a goat's eyes are? Look into mine.

The poem ends elusively, in a teasing evasion: it works like a riddle—you will want an answer, a decision, it says; I will give you the clues from which response may be inferred.

It is a move this poet understands deeply. Refusals and evasions that, in a lesser artist, would seem irritating or tricky seem, in Streckfus, subtle instruction: in tolerance of ambiguity and irresolution, in patience. The wish for an answer, like the wish for stability, is at bottom a wish for self-deception; Streckfus will not honor it.

In that sense, he is something of a moralist. Unmistakably, he is a seeker, his quests and journeys unlike any I have encountered. The reader is less required than invited. And how formidable the delight of accepting, how rare the adventure:

> Here is a wall. The strange empty space above the wall . . .
> what is it for? Here, a little boat, a canopy of silver plastic
> rattling above it.

> Listen to the babe-scare cry of the wind. . . .

And then:

> There's no place for that weapon here. Come on now, you
> have no choice. Trust me.
>
> I'll speak nonsense. You speak truth. We'll see what comes
> of it.

—"AFTER WORDS"

2004

CRUSH / RICHARD SIKEN

This is a book about panic. The word is never mentioned. Nor
is the condition analyzed or described—the speaker is never outside it long enough to differentiate panic from other states. In the
world of *Crush*, panic is a synonym for being: in its delays, in its
swerving and rushing syntax, its frantic lists and questions, it fends
off time and loss. Its opposite is oblivion: not the tranquil oblivion
of sleep but the threatening oblivions of sex and death. The
poems' power derives from obsession, but Richard Siken's manner is sheer manic improv, with the poet in all the roles: he is
the animal trapped in the headlights, paralyzed; he is also the
speeding vehicle, the car that doesn't stop, the mechanism of
flight. The book is all high beams: reeling, savage, headlong,
insatiable:

> . . . Names called out across the water,
> names I called you behind your back,
> sour and delicious, secret and unrepeatable,

the names of flowers that open only once,
shouted from balconies, shouted from rooftops,
or muffled by pillows, or whispered in sleep,
or caught in the throat like a lump of meat.
I try, I do. I try and try. A happy ending?
Sure enough—*Hello darling, welcome home.*

The poem can't stop:

> . . . Names of heat and names of light,
> names of collision in the dark, on the side of the
> bus, in the bark of the tree, in ballpoint pen
> on jeans and hands and the backs of matchbooks
> that then get lost. Names like pain cries, names
> like tombstones, names forgotten and reinvented,
> names forbidden or overused. . . .
>
> —"SAYING YOUR NAMES"

Or, in "Wishbone":

> I'm bleeding, I'm not just making conversation.
> There's smashed glass glittering everywhere like stars.
>   It's a Western,
> Henry. It's a downright shoot-em-up. We've made a
>   graveyard out of the bone white afternoon.

And later:

> Even when you're standing up
> you look like you're lying down, but will you let me kiss your
>   neck, baby?

Do I have to tie your arms down? Do I have to stick my
    tongue in your mouth like the hand of a thief,
  like a burglary . . .

The poems' desperate garrulousness delays catastrophe. Accumulation and reiteration avert some impact, some deadly connection. This is also the way one would address an absence, allowing no pause for the silence that would constitute response.

That Siken turns life into art seems, in these poems, psychological imperative rather than literary ploy: the poems substitute the repeating cycles of ritual for linear progressive time—in *Crush*, the bullet enters the body and then returns to the gun. Cameras are everywhere, and tapes, the means by which an instant can be replayed over and over, manipulated. The poems' tense playbacks and freeze frames—their strategies of control—delineate chilling certainties and immutabilities. Which means, of course, the poems are driven by what they deny; their ferocity attests to the depth of their terror, their resourcefulness to the intractability of the enemy's presence. Everything is a trick, the poems say, everything is art, technology—everything, that is, can still change. This is Siken's way of saying the reverse: in these poems, everything is harrowing and absolute and deadly real:

It was night for many miles and then the real stars in the
    purple sky,
      like little boats rowed out too far,
begin to disappear.
        And there, in the distance, not the promised land,
                but a Holiday Inn,
with bougainvillea growing through the chain link by the
  pool.

The door swung wide: twin beds, twin lamps, twin
        plastic cups
wrapped up in cellophane
                    and he says *No Henry, let's not do this.*
Can you see the plot like dotted lines across the room?
        Here is the sink to wash away the blood,
here's the whiskey, the ripped-up shirt. Here is the tile of the
        bathroom
                floor, the disk of the drain
                        punched through with holes.
Here is the boy like a sack of meat, here are the engines,
        the little room
            that is not a room,
    the Henry that is not a Henry, the Henry with a needle and
        thread,
                hovering over the hollow boy passed out
                        on the universal bedspread.

Time passes:

        The bell rings, the dog growls,
    and then the wind picking up, and the light falling,
            and the window closing tight against the dirty rain.

And later:

    He puts his hands all over you to keep you in the room.
                It's night. It's noon. He's driving. It's happening
    all over again.

                · · ·

I've been in your body, baby, and it was paradise.
I've been in your body and it was a carnival ride.

—"THE DISLOCATED ROOM"

If panic is his groundnote, Siken's obsessive focus is a tyrant, the body. His title, *Crush*, suggests as much. In the dictionary, among the word's many meanings, "to press between opposing bodies so as to break or injure; to oppress; to break, pound or grind." Or, as a noun, "extreme pressure." Out of this cauldron of destruction, its informal meaning: infatuation, the sweet fixation of girl on boy. In Siken, boy on boy. In its fusion of the erotic and the life-threatening, the inescapable, *Crush* suggests *The Story of O*, although bondage here is less literal. Sometimes the poems that most sharply delineate this obsession work from the moment outward and backward; in waves, sometimes we get eerie flashbacks, succinct, comprehensive, premonitory, as in the first section of "A Primer for the Small Weird Loves," lines that predict and summarize a life:

> The blond boy in the red trunks is holding your head
>   underwater
> because he is trying to kill you,
>   and you deserve it, you do, and you know this,
>   and you are ready to die in this swimming pool
> because you wanted to touch his hands and lips and this
>   means
>
>   your life is over anyway.
>   You're in the eighth grade. You know these things.
>   You know how to ride a dirt bike, and you know how to
>   do long division,
>   and you know that a boy who likes boys is a dead boy, unless
>   he keeps his mouth shut, which is
>   what you didn't do,

because you are weak and hollow and it doesn't matter anymore.

For a book like this to work, it cannot deviate from obsession (lest its urgency, in being occasional, seem unconvincing). Books of this kind dream big; they trust not only what drives them but the importance of what drives them. When they work, as Plath's *Ariel* works, they are unforgettable; they restore to poetry that sense of crucial moment and crucial utterance that may indeed be the great genius of the form. But the problems of such undertakings are immense; Plath's thousand imitators cannot sustain her intensity or her resourcefulness. The risk of obsessive material is that it may get boring, repetitious, predictable, shrill. And the triumph of *Crush* is that it writhes and blazes while at the same time holding the reader utterly: "sustaining interest" seems far too mild a term for this effect. What holds is sheer art, despite the apparent abandon. Siken has a brilliant sense of juxtaposition, a wily self-consciousness, an impeccable sense of timing. He can slip into his hurtling unstoppable sentences and fragments of viciously catty wit, passages of epigrammatic virtuosity:

> Someone once told me that explaining is an admission of failure.
> > I'm sure you remember, I was on the phone with you, sweetheart.
>
> —"LITTLE BEAST"

> . . . This is where the evening splits in half, Henry, love or death. Grab an end, pull hard, and make a wish.
>
> —"WISHBONE"

Some of these have a plangency and luster we haven't expected:

> Every story has its chapter in the desert, the long slide from
> kingdom
>   to kingdom through the wilderness,
>   where you learn things, where you're left to your
>   own devices.
>   —"DRIVING, NOT WASHING"

Inevitability and closure haunt these poems; the deferred, the fated—impending loss and deserved punishment—suffuse every line. The poems draw a feverish energy from what they don't really believe: even as the speaker lives his strategies, he doesn't believe in his own escape. Not every poem operates this way. Siken occasionally locates a poem in loss as enacted, not implicit, event. These are among his most beautiful poems, their capitulations heartbreaking in the context of prolonged animal struggle against acknowledgment. One begins the book, positioning the reader as complicitous:

> Tell me about the dream where we pull the bodies out of the
> lake
>   and dress them in warm clothes again.
>   How it was late, and no one could sleep, the horses
>   running
>   until they forget that they are horses.
>   It's not like a tree where the roots have to end
>   somewhere,
>   it's more like a song on a policeman's radio,
>   how we rolled up the carpet so we could dance,
>   and the days

were bright red, and every time we kissed there was
   another apple

                        to slice into pieces.
Look at the light through the windowpane. That means it's
   noon, that means
      we're inconsolable.
         Tell me how all this, and love too, will ruin us.
These, our bodies, possessed by light.
                  Tell me we'll never get used to it.

                        —"SCHEHERAZADE"

Tell me, the poet says, the lie I need to feel safe, and tell me in
your own voice, so I believe you. One more tale to stay alive.

It is difficult, given the length of Siken's characteristic poems, to convey in an introduction a sense of their cumulative,
driving, apocalyptic power, their purgatorial recklessness. In
other ways, this introduction has been difficult; because of the
poems' interconnectedness, the temptation has been to quote
everything. Such difficulty is, in itself, praise of the work.

We live in a period of great polarities: in art, in public policy,
in morality. In poetry, art seems, at one extreme, rhymed good
manners, and at the other, chaos. The great task has been to infuse
clarity with the passionate ferment of the inchoate, the chaotic.

Siken takes to heart this exhortation. *Crush* is the best example I can presently give of profound wildness that is also
completely intelligible. By Higginson's report, Emily Dickinson
famously remarked, "If I read a book and it makes my whole
body so cold no fire can warm me, I know that it is poetry. If I
feel physically as if the top of my head were taken off, I know
that it is poetry. These are the only ways I know it. Is there any
other way?"

She should, in that remark, have shamed forever the facile, the decorative, the easily consoling, the tame. She names, after all, responses that suggest violent transformation, the overturning of complacency by peril.

In practice, this has meant that poets quote Dickinson and proceed to write poems from which will and caution and hunger to accommodate present taste have drained all authenticity and unnerving originality. Richard Siken, with the best poets of his impressive generation, has chosen to take Dickinson at her word. I had her reaction.

2005

GREEN SQUALL / JAY HOPLER

Before poetry began pitching its tent in the library and museum, before, that is, mediated experience supplanted what came to seem the naïve fantasy of more direct encounter, a great many poems began in the garden.

In the tense final decades of the twentieth century, poets have tended to treat the natural world as a depleted or exhausted metaphor: the old associations, continuity and renewal, like other emblems of hope, seem poignantly remote. Nor do artists seem tempted to resurrect them—they hardly lend themselves to the prevailing tone, to the particular set of tools a generation has systematically developed and enshrined, tools developed to address other kinds of experiences than those nature is presumed to afford. If, recently, disinterest has given way to fierce steward-ship as the environment grows more and more imperiled, if nature threatened and uncertain has been restored to a certain dignity as the mirror of our own precariousness, if the throw-back has become the harbinger, the problem of tone still remains. The vanishing garden currently revived by poets suits a period in which experience is filtered, prismatically, by art and history: it is not so much a real garden as a garden previously real. The inauthentic present suggesting the charged and important past insofar as irony permits.

Irony has become less part of a whole tonal range than a scrupulous inhibiting armor, the disguise by which one modern soul recognizes another. In contemporary practice, it is characterized by acute self-consciousness without analytical detachment, a frozen position as opposed to a means of inquiry. Essential, at every moment, to signal that one knows one is not the first to think or feel what one thinks or feels. This stance is absolutely at odds with the actual sensations of feeling, certainly, as well with the sensations of making—the sense, immediate and absolute, of unprecedented being, the exalted intensification of that fundamental isolation which marks all things mortal.

Green Squall begins and ends in a garden. But no one would mistake Jay Hopler for a poet of another century: he is more mad scientist than naturalist, his exploding Florida garden a formidable outpost of the seasonal garden of English lyric. If the seasonal garden represents cyclical time (the old ideas of renewal and so on), Hopler's obsession is with entropy, its symbol, often, unremitting fertility:

>   And the sky!
> Nooned with the steadfast blue enthusiasm
> Of an empty nursery.
>
> Crooked lizards grassed in yellow shade.
>
> The grass was lizarding,
> Green and on a rampage.
>
> —"IN THE GARDEN"

So the book starts. But "begins" and "ends" seem the wrong terms—*Green Squall* hardly ever leaves its fertile premises. Hard, though, to equal all that flourishing:

1

There is a hole in the garden. It is empty. I envy it.

Emptiness: the only freedom there is
In a fallen world.

2

Father Sunflower, forgive me—. I have been so preoccupied
    with my backaches and my headaches,
With my sore back and my headaches and my beat-skipping
    heart,

I have ignored the subtle huzzah of the date palms and
    daisies, of the blue daze and the date palms—

3

                    Or don't forgive me, what do I care?
I am tired of asking for forgiveness; I am tired of being
    frightened all the time.
I want to run down the street with a vicious erection,
Impaling everything, screaming obscenities
And flapping my arms; *fuck the date palms,*
Fuck the daisies—

4

As a man, I am a disappointment, I know that.
Is it my fault I was born in shadow? Through the banyan
    trees,

An entourage of slovenly blondes
Comes naked and begging—

5

My days fly from me as though from a murderer.
Can you blame them?
Behind us, the house is empty and quiet as light.

What have I done, Mother,
That I should spend my life
Alone?

—"AND THE SUNFLOWER WEEPS FOR THE SUN, ITS FLOWER"

Insouciance and bravura notwithstanding, there is a solitude
in this art as deep as any in American poetry since Stevens. For
all the explosive vitality and wild fantasy, there are almost no
people here. The mother who periodically figures is like Ramon
Fernandez in Stevens's "The Idea of Order at Key West": from
neither is response expected. Ghostly, remote, part imagination,
part memory: behind the appeals and questions to such figures,
another larger question lurks. Beneath "tell me if you know," the
echoing "tell me that you *are*, that you exist."

Stevens, the great master of tropical extrapolation, is the pre-
siding influence. Like Stevens, Hopler combines verbal extrava-
gance and formal invention with the philosopher's profound
inwardness. In *Green Squall*, inwardness is manifest: even the

garden is a courtyard. Impossible, here, not to think of the place where prisoners take their exercise. Despite violent flourishing, Hopler's courtyard is a kind of prison, a place of voluntary entrapment or exile; its occupants aspire to invisibility. As a place, as an idea, utterly distinct from the hospitable earth of sentimental practice.

Hopler's real companions are other forms of life: flowers, dogs, birds. His flowers have an energy the speaker envies, as he envies their resilient obliviousness. Hopler is as far from unconsciousness as any poet I can name, despite his relentless efforts to intensify sensory deprivation. But at least once the courtyard affords the serenity that is the aim of self-deprivation, justifying the speaker's obstinate retreat:

> This morning, still
> And warm, heavy with the smells
>
> Of gardenia and Chinese wisteria,
> The first few beams of spring sun-
>
> Light filtering through the flower-
> Crowded boughs of the magnolia,
>
> I cannot conceive a more genuine,
> More merciful, form of happiness
>
> Than solitude.

—"AUBADE"

More commonly, the view is less sanguine, as in these two sections from the long poem at the center of the book:

6

We Cannot Love the World as It Is

We cannot love the world as it is,
Because the world, as it is, is impossible to love.

We have only to lust for it—
To lust for each other in it—

And, somehow, to make that suffice.

7

Revisited

No, somehow to make *that sacrifice*.
—"OF HUNGER AND HUMAN FREEDOM"

Repeatedly one sees in the stanzas—sometimes even in the phrases—a characteristic psychological progression, most marked in poems of real gusto and high spirits: the initial spurt of energy and animal vigor yields almost immediately to morose woe. Euphoria seems less a precursor of depression than a component of being depressed. Anxiety either aborts or trumps it, the danger of euphoria being how much noise it makes: it threatens to reveal the soul's hiding place. Hopler's stanzas are like runners who charge the starting gate and then, two feet later, sit down in the dust. But the variations within this structure, in poem after poem, are extraordinary. What is more extraordinary, however, is that irony and self-consciousness, both taken to extremes, have not suppressed intensity. Nor has Hopler's devastating bitter wit, his Larkinesque crankiness, suppressed amazing verbal beauty.

His tonal range, like his range of formal strategies, is immense. How exhilarating to discover, in a long-winded period, a poet with a genius for epigram. A number of poems in *Green Squall* do not exceed six lines; others are made up of linked epigrams, bleak pensées connected together in one varied glittering comic gesture. "The Frustrated Angel," for example, with its sly self-contained jibes and deadpan remarks:

> The Angel says I have the quiet confidence and smoldering
> Good looks one usually associates with more confident and
> attractive people.

> A coward's confession—, that's what he thinks my ulcer is.

And later:

> *That's mighty big talk, isn't it, Hopler—coming from a man who
> lives with his mother?*

Reprimand and regret weave through these poems like dark thread. Fantasies of erasure alternate with visions of stasis: Hopler broods over the present as one broods over a diagnosis— it confirms the past as it predicts the future's cold encroaching certainties. But the major mistakes have all been made, the first having been the most dire:

1

> Being born is a shame—

But it's not so bad, as journeys go. It's not the worst one
We will ever have to make. It's almost noon

And the light now clouded in the courtyard is
Like that light one finds in baby pictures: old

And pale and hurt—

And later:

3

    The clouded light has changed to rain.
    The picture—. No, *the baby's* blurry.
      —"THAT LIGHT ONE FINDS IN BABY PICTURES"

Green Squall is a book filled with tardy recognitions and insights. Always we sense, beneath the surface of even the most raucous poems, impending crisis: the terrifying onset of that life long held at a distance. Always bravura is connected to melancholy, fastidious distinctions to wild exuberance, largesse to connoisseurship, self-contempt to uncontrollably erupting hopefulness. Hopler's dreamy obscurities and rapturous effusions share with his more direct speech a refusal to be groomed into uncommunicative cool: they are encoded, not unintelligible. He writes like someone haunted or stalked; he wants, simultaneously, to hide and to end the anxiety of hiding, to reveal himself (in every sense of the word), to give himself away.

Like all art that has a chance to be remembered, *Green Squall* is an account of being. Such helpless authenticity seems rare now. But perhaps it has always been rare. Perhaps it is more accurate to say that the ratio of competent verse to art has, in our time, shifted. Jay Hopler sounds like no one else: there is a kind of dazed surprise in the lines, as though the poet himself didn't know where these riches came from. And excitement of the highest order: you could no more sleep through Hopler than you could sleep through an alarm clock—the pleasure, of course, is hardly comparable. Like all artists, Jay Hopler writes not to report or re-create experience but to create forms that both enact and define it:

1
Not enough effort in the sky for morning.
The only relics left are those long,

Blunt fingers among the multitudinous buds.
How hard it is, we say—

The will to work is laid aside.

2
I have reached no conclusions, have erected no boundaries.
I have rested, drooling at the mouth-hole.

I have imagined bees coming and going.
I have said that the soul is not more than the body.

I've melted my silver for you.
I have strewn the leaf upon the sod.

I have just come down from my father.
I have suffered, in a dream, because of him.

3
Suddenly from all the green in the park,
A small white envelope appears.

As limpid, dense twilight comes,
The center of its patch of darkness, sparkling,

Rises like a moon made of black glass.
Beneath the clouds the low sky glows—

The garden that was never here,
Reveal it to me.

—"A BOOK OF COMMON DAYS"

2006

FRAIL-CRAFT / JESSICA FISHER

The poet Peter Streckfus once remarked that what he loved most in a book of poems was a quality of persistent strangeness— "swimming in the confusion of it" was his phrase for the reader's initial experience. This quality makes, as Streckfus suggests, an environment; it is not a matter of the shrewdly confused surface or of opacity, nor can it be elaborated into a deliberate aesthetic. Rather, one feels that something has been discovered in the language itself, some property or capacity, some tone never before transcribed, whose implicit meanings the poet has found ways to reveal.

Jessica Fisher writes a poetry of this kind, haunting, elusive, luminous, its greatest mystery how plainspoken it is. Sensory impressions, which usually serve as emblems of or connections to emotion, seem suddenly in this work a language of mind, their function neither metonymic nor dramatic. They are like the dye with which a scientist injects his specimen, to track some response or behavior. Fisher uses the senses this way, to observe how being is converted into thinking. The poems move like dreams or spells: momentum, here, seems less a function of will than an evolved form of passivity; it is that condition in which freedom from decision and choice makes possible a unique flowering of attentiveness and reflection. The poems succumb to movement as though it were desire, with its obsessive repetitions and reen-actments, its circularity:

> Because the valley spreads wide, ridged with the signs
> we read; or because what we needed was always at hand—
> reach down and there was a book, there a slipper, there a glass
> of ice cold water. Hopefully we walked
> the paths laid before us, there was a burr-bush,
> there a blue jay, quail and other creatures, too many
> to follow. Where did they go once we lost their lead?
> Which is to say, where did we not go? Quick, quick,
> they called to us, but we heard only the sound
> of our boots on dried leaves, and were mesmerized;
> we spoke to one another of things in the path,
> we chucked to our horses, when we had them,
> and when we had hats we took them in our hands
> and hallooed to the passersby (brahma bull, bright
> green bird) though we were not yet out of the wood,
> instead it closed in around us, deep were its streams
> and the trees thick around and thick together . . .
>
> —"JOURNEY"

Impossible to begin discussion without first saying how beautiful a thing this is with its calm unfolding syntax, its air, common to so many of Fisher's poems, of being not exactly of this time—better perhaps to say not of time at all. This is time from a perspective not yet ours, time simultaneously infinite and momentary, the voice a continuity through mutability. Like Frost's

"Directive," a poem it resembles in its dramatic situation (though the pairing is revelatory mainly in the differences it suggests), "Journey" seems to have slid off the map; it takes place either permanently, without beginning or end, or repeatedly—it takes place, that is, in myth time, in fairy-tale time. The alert floating voice is hard to anchor in a body, though it reports physical actions and sensations. The usual signals of age and gender are utterly absent. A sense of the child's voice comes and goes, but despite its intimacy "Journey" is not a poem of personal history or personal dilemma. "What do you think we dreamt," this voice asks us toward the end, its casual familiarity transforming the reader from reader to companion. The answer reveals nothing of the dreamer's character: this is not a poem that seeks to identify motive or obsession, though like all poems of obsession "Journey" is a ritual. But the catalyst is external, circumstantial. What initiates "Journey" is the fact that these paths exist: "laid before us," the poem says; they allude neither to goal nor to destination. The poem ends in dream; the dream recapitulates experience, which becomes increasingly impossible to separate from dream. Its meaning is not known, though its importance is not doubted.

Some poets conduct themselves as though they were directing traffic; with others one can hardly see any sign of imposed will. Fisher doesn't bully or coerce; her voice confides and drifts and veers, it pieces together impressions: no orders, no laying down of the law. The poems seem almost impersonal, as though their author were a sensibility, not a history. And yet, through even the most mysterious landscapes, this oddly jaunty voice, unplaceable yet distinctly human, this voice with its faintly archaic sound, periodically speaks.

The remarkable music of "Journey" characterizes Fisher's work; it doesn't indicate her range. Some of the best poems in *Frail-Craft* are prose poems. These eerie vignettes inhabit, simultaneously, the dreaming mind and the detached intelligence that operates intermittently within the dream. One of the book's four sections is composed entirely of these poems, but the gesture appears earlier, in the amazing poem that ends the first section like an exploding flock of balloons, a Fellini movie crossed with a very sophisticated children's book. It needs to be read in its entirety; no excerpt can give adequate sense of its ingenious shifts and surreal ebullience, though the opening lines convey something of both:

> Now—the parade. Lions, red, black & yellow. They *never* go anywhere without a drummer, & also have someone to carry extra oranges, & a hat carrier, for when they're tired. If their heads are bare they can be bonked with a stick. . . .

And much later, after many shifts:

> . . . yesterday the sun shone. Mounted police forced the dancers off the street. Really exciting. All the windows in the town were covered with screening for that very event. A good time was had by all. Good dinner, good people, good night.
>
> —"NOW—THE PARADE"

The mainly short poems of section two sustain these energies. They are, all of them, dreams, though they vary widely in their tones, their scenarios. This is a difficult form for poems: most poets seem a touch too proud of their dreams, too aware of their resonances. Fisher has found a way to use this material mainly, I think, because she never steps out of her invented worlds:

> —the dream I stayed with past waking
> in which Pascale sits sewing rabbit fur to glove your hands
> and silently, feet propped on a table, I flay a long strip
> from each thigh to make you boots. The skin peels easily,
> it's like stripping the pale bark from a fallen birch,
> the muscle beneath like the crimson trunk still teeming . . .
>
> —"FLAYED"

Or this:

> A long man came on foot, his hair was long too. He spoke
> above the river. Many people came, so many that his voice
> couldn't reach them all, but I heard it: I climbed a tree just
> behind.
>
> Below me, a woman got to her knees and cried, her hair
> was thin as a bird's first feathers, her mouth made a horrible shape.
> Mother said she must be a sinner, that the words of this man, who
> has held the Christ, pricked her soul like a needle does cloth.
>
> I didn't cry, nor did Daan Nachtegaal—he was in the tree too.
> After the man finished we went back to swordfighting. The
> sinners followed him into the river and drowned.
>
> —"THE SERMON"

The elasticity of the form, the clarity and directness of this voice speaking from within contexts that seem fairly remote precincts of reality, allow Fisher to construct poems larger than might ordinarily seem within the range of a poet of such marked lyric temperament. As its title suggests, "Novella" is a miniature novel: in terms of plot, it begins with the disappearance of the hero. He stays vanished throughout, as though the function of the beloved were to lead the speaker back into imagination, which resurrects and perpetuates the connection. We collude, as readers, in his disappearance: if the wrong were righted, the poem would end. Whereas seeking him confirms his importance and intensifies his charisma. In this sense, "Novella" is also a poem *about* reading, about being lost in, a wanderer in, a text. "What you find when you're lost you can't look for," the poem tells us. The argument being, "you'd have to get lost to find it again." A logic both impeccable and perverse, deeply invested in the condition of being lost. As it did in "Journey," *seeking* in "Novella" means following a path that has been set or created, in this case by François, to François. We can't find him, and he can't get back: "His footsteps, left on the ice, would be gone when he went to retrace them." In these and other poems here, a particular kind of immersion figures: that being lost in which great discoveries are made, the center of one's being if not found at least approached. Always accident and chance are preferred to purpose. And the path, often, is "the lead that led astray." So that seeking, which recurs, seems not at odds with passivity, since chance and accident, like fate, cannot by definition be fixed objectives. Seeking is often being led; in *Frail-Craft* it alludes to depth, not distance.

For all the music, the sensuous detail of Fisher's art, her demeanor is essentially cool, measuring, intellectual—*speculative* may be a more accurate term. When such composure takes on, as it does in a number of shorter poems, explicitly passionate or erotic subjects, what results are poems so pure, so violent, so absolute, they seem like choral laments in Greek tragedy:

> You would think that I go mad with grief
> when the white sails fill and the keel cuts

the waters like a knife honed on whetstone:
that's the way you're taught to interpret these signs—
matted hair, the salt-dirt lines where sweat has run,
hands that feed the mouth but will not wipe it.
But when my love decides to go and then is gone,
I can still taste him, bitter in the throat; I still
feel the weight of his body as he fights sleep.
I do not fight it: on the contrary, I live there,
and what you see in me that you think grief
is the refusal to wake, that is to say, is pleasure:
qui donne du plaisir en a, and so if
when he couldn't sleep in that long still night
you sensed it and woke to show him how
to unfasten each and every button, then it is
promised you, even when he goes—

—"THE RIGHT TO PLEASURE"

What is being in the world like? For American poets in the mid-
to late twentieth century, this has meant, in the main, being in
a single world patrolled by a single intelligence bent on finding
meaning. The poems made by these compulsions have been
essentially dramatic, artificially weighted at the end with insight.
Impatience with these premises, with pat, histrionic endings,
has fueled a poetry more interested in impressions and possibility
than in symbols and conclusions. This poetry wants to explore
experience before it becomes coherent, therefore too rigorously
channeled.

In various ways, many contemporary poets try to inhabit the
earliest possible phase of this process, the point before experience begins to be organized into categories. The willed intensity and inertia of emphatic closure has bred revulsion to any

stage preliminary to, and therefore tainted by, closure. Chaos has seemed increasingly fertile and attractive; the great problem is that chaos embodied in language is not chaos but form; the page cannot contain the void. This does not mean memorable poems have not been made of these ambitions. But such poems are an artifice in their own way, objects with boundaries, not the wind of the infinite.

The word *artifice* is very grim: it cannot suggest our experience of art, principally because it does not suggest the world of feeling that is both the source and object of art. Too often distaste for sentiment, anxiety at the limitations of the self, create contempt for feeling, as though feeling were what was left over after the great work of the mind was finished.

These issues obtain here, partly because Jessica Fisher has a marked taste for experiment: *Frail-Craft* inhabits the concerns of a period, its philosophic and linguistic dilemmas, but it does so with an intensity and suppleness rarely encountered: experiment never deteriorates into complacency.

Her poems are analytic meditations, their variety and beauty manifestations of extraordinary sensitivity to English syntax. She shares with her contemporaries intelligent suspicion of worn forms without being automatically enchanted by the arbitrary. Meaning is here, saturating the lines: this is not meaning like a kite with its neat string of explication attached; neither is it rote repudiation. Many of the poems are exquisite spatially: Fisher likes to use the whole page; her descending accruing shapes mime the sensations of associative thought—phrases seem to flood in from different parts of the mind, different parts of the life. The effect is musical, like the winds taking over from the strings.

This impression is fundamental. A highly trained, probing intelligence shapes this work, accounts for its precision, its shimmering logic that seems to belong more to mathematics than to language. And yet always the crucial impulse of these poems seems not argument but song. In *Frail-Craft*, Fisher has found a way to represent the cascade of sensations we think of as being without slighting the great presences, love and loss and death, that structure our perceptions. More impressively, she has found ways to generate emotional power without insisting on rigid correlation of event to insight. The marvel is how elegant, how whole, these poems are, their fluidity notwithstanding. Robert Hass has talked in this regard about rhythm as the underlying principle of form. His perceptions apply here; what gives Jessica Fisher's work its sense of form, of repose, is her perfection of ear. That repose, with its strange mobility, its accommodation of surprise, is Fisher's particular genius. To enter these poems is to be suspended in them: like dreams, they both surround and elude.

Repeated readings do not diminish this impression. I read *Frail-Craft* many times and felt, each time, the same involuntary relinquishing, the giving over, like someone standing at the edge of a body of water, hypnotized by the patterns of light, the slight shifts of color, and then led, without ever knowing how, deep into the recesses of contemplation, of emotion. The experience is unforgettable:

> For a very long time   we'd been on the road, you bet
>   we were tired of salt-beef, of sinew and the raw
>
>   wings of insects—
>   and so I suppose you can imagine
>   how it felt at last
>   to cross the mountains
>
>
>   And when it's a long time
>   since you've slept
>   in the disturbing softness

                                        of someone's breath
      that tree-body takes you by surprise—
                                    space enough inside
              for most of us, yet
                          all night we each felt all alone there
                                              walking
      from plain to peak to fog   toward the idea of ocean . . .
            —"STEREOGRAPHY: PIONEER'S CABIN, NEAR GROVE"

                                          2007

THE EARTH IN THE ATTIC /
FADY JOUDAH

Definitions of political poetry are as varied, numerous, and absolute as those of the lyric, with this difference: American poets are eager to define the political in a manner that includes themselves, whereas the lyric will tend to be defined as what the poet has cast off. This was not always so, but in the unstable present, political art seems bold, important, serious, whereas the lyric preoccupations with abiding and insoluble dilemmas seem evasive and frivolous. At the heart of these impassioned realignments is the poet's anxiety lest his art be considered a parlor art: specialized, over-refined, the amusement of privilege.

Underlying these disputes and conversations is a devotion to categories: where there are categories, there are hierarchies.

A problem, of course, is that this language of categories is a language of absolutes, opposing the wholly inward-turning gaze to the wholly outward-turning, although such distinctions are, rather, a matter of degree. In the fiction of such oppositions, at one extreme is a poetry preoccupied with rarified inner states, with perception, a poetry inclining to the fretfully solipsistic, as though the world were an irritant. And at the other extreme, a poetry that mistakes holding opinions for thinking, a poetry determined to right wrongs, self-consciously immersed in what George Oppen called "the certainties / Of place / And of time"— at its worst, bombastic and sentimental, dutifully unbeautiful. But the extremes are rare, and poets both politically alert and spiritually attentive have always existed; I think, in recent years, of Oppen—others will find other examples.

The Earth in the Attic confuses these rituals of classification: Fady Joudah is, in one sense, a deeply political artist (though never an artist who writes to manifest or advance convictions) and, in another sense, a luminous aesthete who thinks in nuance, in refinements. He is that strange animal, the lyric poet in whom circumstance and profession (as distinct from will and fashion) have compelled obsession with large social contexts and grave national dilemmas. Under other conditions, one could imagine this elegant austerity, this precision, this dreamy inwardness absorbed entirely in the natural world. But the sky and earth here are the sky and earth of an imperiled country, or the haunted landscapes of a lost homeland. In either case, the present is experienced elegiacally, the atmosphere of legend already permeating it:

> The end of the road is a beautiful mirage:
>
> White jeeps with mottos, white
> And blue tarps where the dust gnaws
> At your nostrils like a locust cloud
> Or a helicopter thrashing the earth,
> Wheat grains peppering the sky.

For now

Let me tell you a fable:

Why the road is lunar
Goes back to the days when strangers
Sealed a bid from the despot to build
The only path that courses through
The desert of the people.

The tyrant secretly sent
His men to mix hand grenades
With asphalt and gravel,
Then hid the button
That would detonate the road.

These are villages and these are trees
A thousand years old,
Or the souls of trees,
Their high branches axed and dangled

Like lynched men flanking the wadis . . .

—"ATLAS"

"A fable" the poem calls what it retells, but the events, the vocabulary, are recent. The landscape is saturated with a narrative
violence, but the poem more closely resembles lyric pastoral than
contemporary political action poem. Violence has passed, but the
earth is changed, its lunar stillness at once beautiful and appalling.

Joudah's position here is that of the outsider, but a particular
outsider, his method less interrogation than identification. What
in other sensibilities might replicate the colonial gesture here

seems spontaneous, necessary, exact. As a Palestinian in the West, as a doctor who practices emergency medicine, as a poet writing in English: for a number of reasons, in a variety of situations, Joudah finds himself not at home, not among his people. *The Earth in the Attic* is a book of exile, its biblical resonances less motif than echo. The poet makes of exile not a special case, a perverse snobbery, but rather a metaphor for current psychic reality, as though that reality were indeed displacement, if not geographically, metaphysically: we are adrift, in elemental ways, from the past with all its theoretically useful lessons; the sense of groundedness, of continuity it sustained has vanished. The perception is not new; the treatment is. Of displacement, in these poems, a kind of community is made. "Atlas" ends on a recognition, a tacit gesture of welcome, cautious but potentially inclusive—of the poet, obviously, but also of the reader:

> This blue crested hoopoe is whizzing ahead of us
> From bough to bough,
> The hummingbird wings
>
> Like fighter jets
> Refueling in midair.
>
> If you believe the hoopoe
> Is good omen,
>
> The driver says,
> Then you are one of us.

At the deepest level, the fissure cannot be repaired, though human connection—in friendship, in the ministries of medical aid, in love—does what it can. But the sense of deprivation and longing persist: when Fady Joudah dreams, when he falls in love, nearly always the simile involves the word *home*, a restoration and an arrival. One of the most moving poems, "Proposal," is such a dream:

> I see Haifa
> By my father and your father's sea,
> The sea with little living in it,
> Fished out like a land.

The poem ends:

> And the sea, each time it reaches the shore,
> Becomes a bird to see of the land
> What it otherwise wouldn't.
> And the wind through the trees
> Is the sea coming home.

A longing for community may enact itself as curiosity, even as self-protection re-creates distance. Many figures move through these poems, some familial, some strangers, some briefly but intimately known: the men and women who move through a clinic, a population characterized by crisis and transience. In Fady Joudah's quick portraits, each is utterly individual, stark, occasionally comic. These portraits share a refusal of the lingering analytic rumination (which might change them from living people into narcissistic projections)—"Not *why*, but *how*," Joudah says elsewhere, "A humility of science":

> One of the drivers ran over the neighbor's ducks
> The neighbor demanded compensation
> For the post-traumatic stress disorder he accurately anticipates

Do you know what it's like
To drive on roads occupied
By animal farms: you cannot tell
Who killed who or how
Many ducks were there to begin with

—"MOON GRASS RAIN" (6)

Today, I yelled at three old women
Who wouldn't stop bargaining for pills they didn't need
One wanted extra
For her grandson who came along for the ride

—"MOON GRASS RAIN" (8)

Or this, like many similar moments in the shorter poems:

The carpenter
Dying of cancer in a hospital bed
Saying, god, I know
You've given me misfortune

But when I get up there
There'd better be a damn
Good reason for it,
I've got nothing against trees.

—"AN IDEA OF RETURN"

Fady Joudah's gift for swift, telling detail, for image-making, shows itself in other ways—as observation of nature, as expanded psychological portrait. In their particulars, if not in their movement, the poems seem analogues for photographs. But images here perform a critical psychological (as opposed to aesthetic) function: each image makes a stable referent, an iconic substitute for what is lost. For the same reasons, toward the same result, Joudah's model is less the allegory than the folktale, his language a language in which the anecdotal human past is stored, renewed, and affirmed in the retellings. So, too, the chilling testimony of landscape becomes in language fixed, permanent, a means of both affirming and sustaining outrage.

Though an image may *suggest* (in which sense it is not static), it is neither dramatic nor narrative. It follows that poems made of such building blocks move associatively, from image to image, fixed point to fixed point. But in Joudah's work, this movement is neither a buffeted reactiveness (which is passive) nor a meditative rambling (which lacks agenda). In their purposefulness and economy, these lyrics resemble scientific proofs, but proofs written in an utterly direct and human language; in their implicit drivenness, their wish to change the reader as the poet has been changed, the poems acquire a dramatic intensity image-making does not usually produce. "Pulse" means to take us beyond naïveté, to equip us with the poet's informed gaze, or the doctor's registering of every detail, "collecting evidence" (in Hugh Seidman's wonderful phrase). Such seeing and recording have moved far beyond the reeling, self-regarding drama of shock into some more profound, more responsive attentiveness. "Pulse" needs to be read whole, but every section gives indication of its accumulative power:

> On the night of the accident
> That flipped over the military truck
>
> Cracking many teenage bones, there was a wedding.
> The family blazed the air,
>
> Bullets came down
> Into the groom's chest.

Last night we heard a *Pop.*
One of us shouted *Wow* in her sleep.

Another, awake and laughing, said:
Here goes the bride

And the dowry: cash
That looks like human remains . . .

—"PULSE (7)"

He fired, they fired, into the air.

By now the slight jerk in the listener's neck
Is a Rilkean gazelle in her water spring.

Toddlers still take off in terror, besieged
By calm in the mother's voice.

—"PULSE (8)"

Halimah's mother did not seem aware Halimah was dying.

You should have seen Halimah fight her airlessness
Twisting around for a comfortable spot in the world.

    . . .

                . . . Halimah
Died of a failing heart
Early this dawn, her mother, with tears now,

Was on the road, twenty steps past me
Before I turned and found her waiting. . . .

—"PULSE (12)"

Certain of the poems here, notably this sequence, seem located in Darfur—impossible to be certain since the place, or places, are not named. This is deliberate, not coy, a way of insisting on the representative or paradigmatic quality of what unfolds. The poems record the survival of the recognizably human under inhuman conditions—in the hands of a lesser writer, this would be unreadable, sententious. But what underlies these poems is fury that the human should be so mercilessly and relentlessly taxed. The tales Fady Joudah tells are the tales of a very recent present, but a present turned, absolutely and suddenly, to long ago:

> Between what should and what should not be
> Everything is liable to explode. Many times
> I was told *who has no land has no sea*. My father
> Learned to fly in a dream. This is the story
> Of a sycamore tree he used to climb
> When he was young to watch the rain.
>
> Sometimes it rained so hard it hurt. Like being
> Beaten with sticks. Then the mud would run red.

The tree is gone—only a fluke that the father isn't. But what he has seen imperils him:

> My brother believed bad dreams could kill
> A man in his sleep, he insisted
> We wake my father . . .
>
> —"SLEEPING TREES"

A sense of religious intensity or necessity emanates from these poems, as though, in the absence of the authenticating earth—where home was—only language remains, having to take on the work of both earth and spirit. It is, here, the single means by which tradition and history (the constructs in which the personal is rooted) can be kept alive. Even the most specific and local details have a lyric timelessness. On the page, incident and description are freshly perceived, quotidian; an underlying imperative transforms them into parables, the patina of time already half acquired before the poem is even complete. The tales have an incantatory quality; they more closely resemble spells than gossip. They are the elemental messages of sleep and art, charged with omen:

> Say I found you and god
> On the same day at the border
> Of words, better two late birds than
>
> The stone that hit them. . . .

The poem ends like this:

> And in the new country,
> Say the hoopoe will still reach us,
>
> Say anything that doesn't wake me
> From my morning sleep,
> My dreams take too long
> And I must finish them.

—"LOVE POEM"

The improvisational, let-me-tell-you-a-story *say* of the opening line, the *say* of *just suppose*, becomes, by the end, imperious, a command rooted not in ego-need but in the authority of dream. These are small poems, many of them, but the grandeur of conception inescapable. Fathers and brothers become prophets, hypothesis becomes dream, simple details of landscape transform themselves into emblems and predictions. The book is impossible to put down, impossible to forget:

> In the calm
> After the rain has bombed the earth
>
> The ants march out of their shelters
> One long frantic migration line
>
> They hit the concrete floor
> Of our dining and living
>
> Space then turn into the shadow
> The wall makes, a straight angle
>
> To the courtyard wreckage of dirt and gravel:
>
> Did they know the wind
> Would airdrop new rations their way?
>
> It's always two or three
> Ants locking their horns to the acid end
>
> Over nothing—it seems
> More than an impulse,
>
> The debris plenty for all.   —"PULSE (10)"

2008

IT IS DAYLIGHT / ARDA COLLINS

Before Eddie Murphy became a movie star, he was a crucial part of one of the several golden ages of *Saturday Night Live*; I am thinking in particular of the beaming malice of Mr. Robinson (aka Mr. Rogers) of "Mr. Robinson's Neighborhood." Here were all the accustomed props to which we parents were unavoidably exposed: the cardigan waiting in the closet (along with the comfy footwear constituting the at-home uniform that separated the outside from the inside); the new word chalked on the handy blackboard (a word that America's children were encouraged to both learn and visualize), the blackboard itself Mr. Rogers's solemn promise to parents that the children committed to his care were not transformed by the trance-inducing hypnotic screen into robots, but rather into readers. Unlike Mr. Rogers, Mr. Robinson was not at home; he was either staging a passive-aggressive refusal to vacate or he was practicing a vocation for hiding out; in either case, his visitors were enraged landlords. For a certain number of years, Fred Rogers's soothing chatter mutated on late-night TV into Mr. Robinson's solitary paranoid ramblings: Mr. Robinson was unwelcome, but Mr. Robinson, for the benefit of all of us former children too hooked or wired to go to sleep, Mr. Robinson was digging his heels in and, crouched under the window, ready to talk, even if talking meant talking to a void.

What these segments have in common with Arda Collins's savage, desolate, brutally ironic first book is the electric excitement of a master performance conducted in a deliberately isolated space, as though isolation were a form of control that promoted fluency. Like Eddie Murphy, Collins has invented a persona: *Welcome to my world*, the first poem seems to say, and for the next ninety-two pages, we are her mesmerized audience—nobody escapes:

> At last, terror has arrived.
> Next door, the house has gone up in flames.
> A woman runs from the burning wreck, her face smeared
> with blood and ashes. She screams that her children are
> kidnapped.
> It's truly exciting, and what more would anyone ask?
> For a rare and beautiful egg to present itself in the grass?
> For sex with the liquor store owner to progress into
> something meaningful?
> You don't know what I've done in front of the mirror.
> I've pulled my shorts up high like a thong. I've walked back
> and forth
> doing little kicks and making faces. I've stopped, I've stared.
> I try to get my mind around the sight of myself. I make a face.
> Of great seriousness. I imagine that I've just received
> a large and upsetting piece of news. Then I look into my eyes.
> Can I guess what I am thinking? Can I tell you what it is?
>
> —"THE NEWS"

It Is Daylight has, to some extent, roots in those long Victorian monologues in which character is developed through manipulation of tone, and a narrative emerges through that character's evasions and juxtapositions. A closer analogy might be the analytic monologue (though Collins's brilliant, sly free associations are far more original than the patient is ever likely to be). Structurally, the poems resemble not adult analysis as much as the work done with children, in which dramatic play augments or provides occasions for speech. The analytic perspective contributes detachment, distance; the self that acts is, here, always at a certain remove, its actions observed with a committed neutrality. Collins talks without interruption (no one is ever present to interrupt); she also performs, exhibits herself. But make no mistake: this is not a book of individual travail and self-exposure. Like the analyst, these poems never stop thinking. Collins's mugging and kicking are the opposite of narcissistic preening; they arise, I think, out of deep confusion. The parading in front of mirrors, like the invisible quotes around "meaningful," like the elliptical memories and tableaux, the fantasies—all dramatize a fundamental vacancy: the hope is that one of these gestures, one of these stories, will seem authentic, representative.

At the heart of the poems' struggles is shame, which results not from something the speaker has done, from action, but rather from *being*, from what she is or what she lacks. Collins's speaker cannot bear to be seen; hence her furtiveness, her preference for enclosed environments (sometimes her fear of light). The private closed spaces that protect this speaker from being seen (while paradoxically freeing her to speak) function in other ways, both contextualizing and mirroring a metaphysical claustrophobia: the bleak fate of being always one person. Sometimes Collins's closed space is not merely contained but barely plausible, the space of a human foot on top of a slice of onion:

As you're standing with the heel of your shoe
on top of some neatly sliced red onion
you might think to yourself, "I'm at onion,"
or, "I'm in onion today." Coming home
in the evening you might see a letter
waiting there, tucked just underneath
the sliced onion. . . .

And later:

. . . That evening, beside the onion,
you write in your journal . . .

As the poem goes on, as less of the world comes in, disorienta-
tion intensifies:

. . . You sleep
on the floor and wake
disoriented and frightened, uncertain if
the heaviness surrounding your sleep is onion
that still permeates your fingers. Day comes
to your estranged bed,
the mood of the bathtub inexplicably
altered . . .

—"WITH A VOICE IN FRONT OF YOU"

Many poems follow the same arc: what begins as reprieve
ends as indictment. The poems are ruled by habit, by ritual, their
speaker less hostage to a specific secret than constrained by the
habit of secrecy, the need to be protected from the unknown.
She understands from the inside the prison of magical thinking;
in one poem, she cannot decide "which way to walk around /
and approach the table / for the best outcome."

Ritual and hiding promise safety; so too does art, which excludes the world, constructing a parallel and at least partially sustaining universe. But art is dangerous, taunting; it exposes insufficiencies; it takes one to the terrible depths one fears:

> Don't put off your shower any more
> listening to Chopin.
> Take the Preludes personally;
> he's telling you that he can describe a progression
> that you yourself have been unable to see,
> shapely, broad light at one-thirty,
> evening traveling up a road,
> an overcast day as gentle bones.
> Don't remember the music;
> remember it as something obvious
> that you are compelled, doomed, to obscure
> and complicate. You erase it twice.
> The first time
> as you listened, unable
> to have it,
> the second time
> as you were unable
> to remember it.
> Angry with Chopin,
> *what does he know? . . .*

And finally:

> Listen to him describe what you would be like
> if you were blind, sitting in a chair, at a wake, the days short,
>   that there might be nothing
>   else, night,

content, unable, unwishing, to recall desire, or sight.

—"NOT FOR CHOPIN"

This locked-in quality, the inescapability of self, manifests temporally as well as spatially. *It Is Daylight* constructs a universe in which time doesn't pass. In one poem, the accident of stepping on an onion elaborates itself into a version of Dickinson's letter to the world. And in the book as a whole, time has ceased, though day flips into night and back again, like two aspects of paralysis. Because the self doesn't change, because it is exposed to nothing that would change it, time seems not to pass. The last poem recapitulates the first, with its burning house and kidnapped or murdered child—all these poems later, we're still frozen in front of the television, watching these same images. Or this is a version of the onion-world: a book-length account of a moment. The passion not to be seen is played back in the poems as intense seeing, voyeurism; the "estranged bed," i.e., the world, intrudes, via television, into Collins's Skinner boxes.

But no description of prevailing atmosphere does justice to Collins's achievement. How has she managed to make, out of stasis, a book so intensely dramatic? The obstacles are obvious: if the voice deviates too much from narrowness, then narrowness seems willed, artificial; the reader's belief falters. But the obsessive precisions that immobility is likely to produce seem, by definition, repetitive, boring. Collins's solutions are subtle: like a great actor, she stays in character; what moves is the camera:

> It's not happiness, but something else; waiting
> for the light to change; a bakery.

> It's a lake. It emerges from darkness into the next day
> surrounded by pines.

There's a couple.

It's a living room. The upholstery is yellow and the furniture
   is walnut.
They used to lie down on the carpet

between the sofa and the coffee table, after the guests had left.

The cups and saucers were still.

Their memories of everything that occurred took place
with the other's face as a backdrop and sometimes

the air was grainy like a movie about evening, and sometimes
   there was an ending
in the air that looked like a scene from a different beginning,

in which they are walking.

It took place alongside a scene in which one of them looks up
   at a brown rooftop
early in March. The ground hadn't softened.

One walked in front of the other breathing.
The other saw a small house as they passed and breathed. The
   reflections in the windows

made them hear the sounds on the hill: a crow, a dog, and
   branches—
and they bent into the hour that started just then, like
   bending to walk under branches.

—"LOW"

As single moments expand to fill a page, memories (the *before* and *after* absolute but the transition nearly invisible) turn dreamy, partial. They seem less comprehensive anatomies than gestures or sketches, searches for analogues and tonal equivalents. By virtue of being past change, the world of memory, like the four walls to which Collins clings, makes an alternative to the outside world—here also time is banished, its repeated passage, phrase by phrase, controlled by the mind. But the world of memory remains strangely incomplete, elusive, mysterious, as though the poet cannot quite say what occurred, only what feelings were generated. The search is for exact emotion, not narrative fact—fact, to Collins, is suspect, a disguise; only nuance, the suggestiveness of a phrase, seems to her reliable, trustworthy. In a lesser poet this privileging of the evanescent over the concrete might be a dangerous predilection, but Collins's animal accuracies, her instinct and intelligence, never fail her. The respite of memory rewrites the schism in the self. The self in the present, always both performing and taking notes, becomes the self that acted and the self that remembers, the shift in tense making each self potentially whole. This, together with the atmosphere of searching or incompleteness, makes, despite the poem's sadness, a model for hope. If something can end (the *before* of *before* and *after*), something can begin; time can begin, feeling can begin.

Readers of these poems may think of Berryman's *Dream Songs*, though Berryman is more haunted by guilt than by shame. It is interesting to remember that those Dream Songs were followed by prayer: *Love and Fame* ends with a series of addresses to the Lord, which continue to seem to me among that poet's most moving work. Collins has woven theological argument (if not prayer) into her book; its thematic prominence intensifies as the book evolves. God is, in many instances, the only other presence, too mysterious and pervasive for any pronoun, divine authority confirmed by silence:

> I put my hands on the table
> and spread them, like
> "here's all ten." There's nothing on it,
> on the table,
> so I found that out.
> What did you do today?
> I ask god.
> God doesn't say anything.
> I don't say anything else. . . .

And later:

> We stay like that
> for a long time,
> and I mean a really long time.
> That's one thing,
> god is the only one
> who would do that.

—"HEAVEN"

This conversation continues elsewhere with fervor: "The universe is on earth," Collins writes, "unexpurgated / soil and frost." And the lament that has been fended off finally surfaces, the persona splintering into the third person. "Dawn" is longer than many of these poems, but its individual sections suggest, in their terse completeness, utter despair:

> He slit a zoo
> full of animals.

It was only one calf.
It turned out to be a person,
not a calf. The calf
made sounds.
Blood filled the grass,
the end of winter. . . .

—"DAWN (I)"

And then, from this persona-once-removed, an intelligence two voices away from the poet, comes authentic grief, what is left when rage is played out:

Gentle, painful sound,
it's coming from his face.
He doesn't want to talk,
hates the air; it moves towards the same things,
beautiful night,
beautiful night again, best missed
from afar. . . .

—"DAWN (II)"

Collins is hopeless on principle: fear of disappointment combined with a vivid sense of helplessness have produced terror of action. For action, she substitutes memory and fantasy. Scrupulous inertia cannot, however, suppress an imagination so violently alive. The self that hides out is in fact a guerilla fighter; the atmosphere of the book is fierce engagement and despair, not placid resignation. The long, sometimes fragmentary poems of the book's second half do not represent disintegration. As paralysis and stasis substitute for wholeness or coherence, fragmentation manifests mobility. "Dawn"'s separation of rage from grief, as well as its somnambulistic quality, prepare for

"Neptune." Here every line is succinct, but sequence, which earlier seemed fated, decided a priori, seems suddenly in flux. The beautiful phrases have a kind of stunned quality, a sense of being led forward, which oddly seems, in this context, freedom, since its alternative is adamant will wholly bent on repudiation:

> We pass the day in March of being in the cemetery and
> eating a burger.
>
> The air is made out of statues and dead people.
>
> This is why we have sex together.
>
> Did I show you this?
>
> It passed through the particles.
>
> The shadows of a continent passed over
> us like the shadow of a cloud over a body of
> water.

And later:

> The upstairs room in the summer is soft and quiet.
>
> Rain dims coming in the night outside.
>
> It is real that it is quiet, and the noise
> is away from here, inside the train.
>
> When I lie next to you I miss the world.

This is a book of dazzling modernity as, say, Jim Jarmusch seems modern: caustic, pithy, ruthlessly sharp-witted and keen-eyed, restless, devoid of that taste for rhetorical splendor that turns so easily stodgy. If the persona here is well-defended, the larger point is that these defenses are among Collins's subjects. I know no poet whose sense of fraud, the inflated emptiness that substitutes for feeling, is more acute. Collins sounds always like a particular person, but she is, here, tracking a culture.

Within its devised constrictions, this voice has the freedom to say anything. The result is a book of astonishing originality and intensity, unprecedented, unrepeatable:

> There was snow on the apples
> somewhere.
> You're at home.
> It's getting dark out, rain
> makes the cars louder. Nobody
> seems to be driving
> the cars. Someone has arranged
> for them to be there going by,
> six o'clock. Someone has made
> the sound of air in the room louder.
> God? you say, but not aloud. Since
> there is no god, you have to be
> both you and god. . . .

The TV's on, "something about a fire / and a kidnapped boy." The hypnotic story unfolds again, the mother's anguish this time more detailed, more relentless. And then:

> . . . Her voice makes you hungry.
> You ask god if god

is hungry, and god is. You ask god
what you should do
for dinner, and god reminds you
that you have turkey burgers
in the freezer, and some broccoli.
You'll get up
with creases on your face.
The windows will be dark. You'll
go take the burgers out
and separate them with a knife.
They'll be slippery and frozen, and
you'll think of driving on an
icy road; and then
you'll put them in foil under
the broiler and start the water
for the broccoli, and take out
a plate for yourself, and get
the salt and pepper, and by
that time god will have left.
God's going to a dinner
where they're having lamb chops
and veal stuffing with
roasted almonds and fig sauce and
Brussels sprouts buttered with pistachios.
And after, they're going to have
pear clafoutis behind a velvet curtain
and drive their skulls into the center of a diamond.

—"SNOW ON THE APPLES"

2009

JUVENILIA / KEN CHEN

Poetry students in the 1960s were fond of a game based on renga, the Japanese collaborative form that alternates stanzas of seventeen and fourteen syllables. The classical form depends on the principles of link and shift, what Basho called "refraining from stepping back," each individual stanza both connected to and evolving from its predecessor. In Stanley Kunitz's twentieth-century classroom, the poem rotated clockwise from student to student; for "poem" read a piece of paper folded backward from the top, so that each of us saw only that stanza directly preceding the one we were about to write, which we hoped would be both boldly formal and mathematically perfect. The whole, to which the increasing thickness of the fold alluded, was unknowable: its progressive temporary vanishing facilitated our Basho-like refraining—there was no world to step back into. Narrative, trajectory, sustained meditation around a single set of ideas, these conventions by which we practiced a form, were precluded by the renga's methodical opacity; it restricted from view nearly everything that came before. Instead we made a chain of associations, each moment connected only to the two adjacent, making the last stanza often entirely remote from the first.

Retrospectively, a poem of this kind acquired a distinct psychological aura: it suggested a mode of being characterized by disconnection, requiring a compensatory intensity of focus on immediate detail. In place of a single governing idea or story, we relied on inference and improvisation: the past was buried or denied (folded over) though it continued imperiously to shape the present. Coexisting with heightened sensitivity to the moment was a constant intuition of something vast or crucial, veiled, but still limiting or directing choices. One analogue to this state might be the immigrant experience, what Ken Chen calls "the Peking opera soundtrack of my childhood."

Strange passengers in a stationary Acura, in what might be a parking lot, might also be a film lot: a father who drops the keys in the toilet, a mother "like the moon which rents light from the past," a small boy, an ancient Chinese poet (long dead), and, floating through the scene like a bit player in a crowd scene who goes where needed, an equally remote dreamlike grandfather who seems a character in a surreal gangster movie:

> *The suitcase open on the bed.*
> *My grandfather is packing up his organs.*
> *When he is done, he takes a taxi to my grandmother's house for*
> *supper.*
> *Exits the empty car to Taipei alley.*
>
> *Dissolve. Now the Los Altos lot.*

So did you listen to him, my Father, taking his keys out of the ignition. You should become a lawyer but your grandfather says anything is fine. As long as you're the best.

My Father stays, my Mother stays silent. I sit and suck my thumb.

I saw your painting. It was beautiful, my Mother says to Wang Wei, restrained beside me by backseat-belt and street-light world . . .

. . .

California moon not glow—or as the translation might say, ir-radiates instead . . .

And later:

. . . You're young, my Father says,
I'm not sure to me or Wang Wei . . .

. . .

. . . and then Wang Wei:

Red hearts in the southern country.
Spring comes with stems enlarging.
I didn't know you two were still together.

We're not, my Father says. . . .

—"MY FATHER AND MOTHER DECIDE MY FUTURE
AND HOW COULD WE FORGET WANG WEI?"

The dead poet, dutifully dragged into the twentieth century, is no more adrift than the other hostages, including the nascent poet, representative of the first generation's amnesia. In their experience, the present does not build on the past; it replaces the past. Normal evolutionary modifications yield to something more radical and violent, the early self less changed than buried, its memories incapable of mutation or incorporation. Memories of this kind, of a lost world, are frozen: they exist independent of the present, in no relation to it. On the surface, the present may seem to outsiders enviably free, the past not close enough to reproach it or dictate to it. In fact, the present is haunted or crippled precisely because it cannot contain the past in a way that might change one's perception of it.

In this world, cryptic non sequitur and silence often substitute for disclosure. The alternative: the child poet comes to his vocation for speech unwittingly, body-first, via his "garrulous rash that tells my skin all the secrets of my body." He has, by now, instead of one car, two households; instead of a dead poet, a sibling:

> He asked about his parents, why they split up in the first place, what were they like when they were his age? My father—my mom's roommate from thirty years ago reveals—would mill around my mother's place every day, inspect the grass . . .

But in general, "They don't talk about these things, my parents, who are as talkative as trees." What does talk is the world outside the family; doctors and waiters are mines of information, not all of it useful:

> At the doctor's office, I watch the doctor's wall. A new flu bulletin! Have good posture!

Or:

> The waiter at Jade Pavilion thinks my mother is my sister. The waiter walks up and says, "It doesn't matter that no one is

home, we still love her." He pours the tea and asks, "What good is eternal youth if no one loves you?"

And later:

> She takes me to the last doctor. Doctor number seven. Who jerks
> his finger in the air and says "Ah, Penicillin! Penicillin muddies
> the waters!" and his hair plugs rustle like a lawn in suburbia.
>
> —"THERE ARE TWO TYPES OF TREES IN WINTER,"

Juvenilia is not, however, in its primary impulses autobiographical. Ken Chen is far too sophisticated and ambitious a poet to have written a local or sentimental book. The power and originality of this collection owe in part to Chen's use of immigrant displacement as a metaphor for the adult's relation to his childhood, or origins. No accident that the child is trapped in the backseat with the dead poet: over and over in these poems, the lost homeland corresponds to the vanished world of childhood and the adult speaker to the immigrant. The first world is gone: no one who knew it will talk about it. What survives is a vivid (sometimes paralyzing) conviction that, like the folded-over stanzas, it determines the present.

"The Invisible Memoir" is a tour de force on these themes; the defining thread of abandonment holds together diverse forms:

> My gold sword sunk into the ground.
> My spirit lost among the long weeds.
> Then in the cool night. Then in the quiet sky. Then the
> moon blossoming open.
> My mind goes back to those old hallways, but now only
> the light glows hollow on the waters of Ch'in-huai.

Uncle's house—the happiest time of my life.

Staying—fate
3rd daughter
Grandfather—divorce
Your son is having an affair
The same price
I pay for the son, you pay for the daughter

So the poem proceeds, a collage of exquisite, elusive translations, strange lists and outlines in which an entire human drama is contained, conversations, opinions, homilies, verdicts, scenes:

> I sit with my sister on my grandmother's couch, where we stare at the coffee table and chew dried sour plums and wafers of Chinese candy, like a pink roll of pennies. My mother would measure our height against our grandmother, who with her husband had fled Beijing for Taipei . . . When my mother was homesick, she thought of Taiwan, unlike her mother who thought of China. My grandmother had acquired a patience that wanted nothing—a sort of contented despair. . . .

"The Invisible Memoir" tells one person's story implicitly; explicitly it is, if not exactly dynastic, a portrait of a culture. The deliberate blurring and overlapping of narrative voices point to thematic recurrences and repetitions. Here, as throughout the book, the first-person pronoun is markedly mobile, only occasionally attached to the artist or his persona. Chen's method is unique: a sort of narrative through excision (the formal correlative of discretion) like a diary with pages torn out, or an account of a complicated past thought to be suitable for a child's ears, the disturbing material prominently deleted. The fragments that exist have to count for a great deal, for everything. Hence the coaching, sometimes by the poet, sometimes by one of the other figures (though it is not always clear who speaks): "Fate is a trap," we are reminded, "but context is dynamic." And a general textbook for living: "Don't gossip / Live in the past." Beyond virtuosity, there is in this (as in many of Chen's poems) a resonant, pervasive echoing, the sense of an earlier language underlying the English lines, faintly distorting them or shifting emphasis. (A striking example of this occurs in "Taipei Novel," one section of which ends with a strangely unforgettable line: "'When I am alone, I feel penitent, my heart damp like cold metal.'" It took me several readings to register the fact that the line is a perfect seventeen syllables, a linear haiku. In other words, the embedded past.)

The blurred identities and boundary confusions of "The Invisible Memoir" take other forms in this book, sometimes direct, comic, and sometimes, as in the love poems, sustained, so that love becomes a kind of quicksand, dissolving individuality. There seems sometimes only the haziest boundary between self and other, self and world:

> She said to her husband, "Last night
> my life was so quiet that my feelings were audible.
> When the phone rang, I thought it was my heart."

Elsewhere, this blurring produces a false reasoning, cause and effect hopelessly intertwined:

> And the waters swallow him—are like the tears you shed.

Then he must not be swimming, for there were no tears . . .

—"TAIPEI NOVEL"

The protagonist, like the reader, must play detective, sniffing out essential facts. Ordering them is another issue.

If it does not simply create panic, the absence of apparent causal relations, together with the scale and frequency of change, stimulates analytic capacities: what experience and memory cannot supply, intelligence infers or pieces together. Pattern and cause can be hypothesized. Chen is obsessed, though, with the defects of this process: logic, which is synthetic, cannot substitute for knowledge; the passion invested in logic mirrors the voids and gaps of memory—the more crucial the gaps, the more passionate the stake in logic.

Ken Chen is a lawyer by education, but these tendencies do not simply reflect training in law. Rather, the habits of mind and disposition that make an effective lawyer (and predispose someone to seek this training) make, in an artist, art of this kind: on the surface, cool, fastidious, obsessive; underneath, daring, relentless. Reasoning is taken to a level of scrupulousness that seems a new form of surrealism:

> Love is like tautology in the same way *like* is like tautology. Both are technologies with which we can turn one thing into another. *Like* for example turns an object around until we realize that what we had thought was a moon had actually been something else entirely—a pearl perhaps . . . Love too is about turns. It begins with turning my head to meet your eye and ends when I turn away from you, lost . . . The middle of love— when we forget that love is what describes us—occurs when I turn to you for everything: to learn how to sleep, to remind

myself that yes I too possess a body and slowly it seems life conveys forward only so I have something to tell you at dinner. Time passes and I know you so well that these two terms—I and You (henceforth, "U")—grow indivisible, are the same . . . Friendship is an expression; love is an equation.

Yet even equations can be unhappy. . . .

The poem goes on to enact a series of crises and failures of feeling, abstract but recognizable, the symbols increasingly baroque, increasingly poignant. The end returns to the simplicities of the beginning:

I call you up to tell you this, but no one answers the phone. Should I go home to see you? I do. There is no U. I is only me, me without you. There is a word for this. When there is only I, when I equals I—we call this an identity.

—" 'LOVE IS LIKE TAUTOLOGY IN THE SAME WAY *LIKE* IS LIKE TAUTOLOGY' "

The confusion love creates with its overeagerness to replace the orphan self with a composite self is partly a confusion of conflicting extreme responses. Love creates feelings both ecstatic and terrifying—a composite self, a "U" or union, mends the wounds of childhood; it also contributes to its obsolescence; the past vanishes in being healed.

Bravura poems work here because there is, at the book's heart, such deep sadness, such wistfulness, such piercing awareness of irreconcilable, immutable needs. Likewise the aphorisms, which in other hands might seem trivial, an exercise in willed charm: these blossom, late in the collection, into a string of pithy, preemptive one-liners that both initiate and end conversations. Sometimes one hears the tone in which a parent silences a child:

> Longing would be so much easier without the other person obstructing it.

And:

> Just because you are the victim does not mean that you are not the perpetrator.

And:

> Why do we cover our mouths in embarrassment? Once we have seen the fangs we can never forget them.
> —"THE CITY OF HABITS"

Some of these moments are ascribed to Confucius, the father of all pith:

> How I have gone downhill! It has been such a long time since I have dreamt of the Duke of Chou.

And in the end, the great man by the river:

> What passes away is, perhaps, like this. Day and night it never lets up.
> —"TAIPEI NOVEL"

These moments occur in a long anecdotal account of an affair, doomed, filled with imbalances, the lovers meeting in the one place, at the one time in which they can come together. The dreamlike result makes a poem in which each moment seems to be memorialized as it occurs.

Great sophistication and high style often flourish at the expense of emotional range. It may be more accurate to say that they are strategies to mask a deficit. The miracle of this book is the degree to which Ken Chen manages to be exhilaratingly modern (anti-catharsis, anti-epiphany) while at the same time never losing his attachment to voice, and the implicit claims of voice: these are poems of intense feeling; they have isolated and dramatized the profound dilemma of the adult's relation to childhood in poems of riveting intelligence and sharp wit and austere beauty.

Reading for a competition such as this involves reading very few books that are not well made. But current systems of education and standards of judgment have tended to produce bodies of work in which a kind of airbrushed polish obscures eccentricity and real distinction. Imagine, among a hundred-odd collections, many of them impressive, coming on a book called *Juvenilia*, with its delicious knowingness and sly collusive irony: the title alone staked a flag at the edge. If this is juvenilia, it seems to say, the earth is flat. Or, alternatively: this is juvenilia in that I, the poet, am young; then imagine the work of my maturity—

Here clearly was a poet who felt it was not enough for him to be good or even brilliant in one of the period manners—here was someone who meant to be individual, electric. The scale of the gift is more than equal to the dare. Like only the best poets, Ken Chen makes with his voice a new category:

> Your son? asks Wang Wei. He has seen me and become
> real, as though a ghost could die into a man. Not the
> monk you quite expect, Wang Wei wears a cowboy's

deadened face and stares at you not unlike an establishing
shot. . . .

. . .

And Wang Wei asks Who are you? And my Father says
Decide.

—"MY FATHER AND MY MOTHER DECIDE MY FUTURE
AND HOW COULD WE FORGET WANG WEI?"

2010

RADIAL SYMMETRY /
KATHERINE LARSON

The human fascination with beauty has produced many acts of tribute and imitation but relatively few insights, possibly because what transpires in the presence of beauty occurs in a mind initially mesmerized or stunned. Other sensations follow, none of them articulate: first a rush of excitement, this succeeded by a feeling of arrival, of completeness, and, with this new completeness, insatiability—the enslaved attention refuses to relinquish its object. The hand (for example) cannot turn the page.

This power to stun the mind has diminished the prestige of beauty in literary discourse. It compels awe, and awe is well known for its capacity to silence. Here is nothing of the sort of puzzle or dilemma the mind prefers. Quite the opposite: beauty seems a sort of all-purpose solution to everything, obviating the debate and argument by which the mind is energized. In consequence, it disappears from debate: by both poets and critics, it is mentioned offhandedly or apologetically, as an incidental virtue or mild defect, unlikely to advance philosophical understanding. It exists—serene, impervious—beyond or apart from the vicissitudes of fashion; it cannot be achieved in the laboratories of ingenuity or craft. Miraculous, and also patently at odds with the play of intellect that (no matter how labored or how trivial) monopolizes contemporary attention and stimulates elaborate response. Numinous and clear, the beautiful offends the mind with its quality of self-sufficiency or finality.

Nowhere is this schism between public approbation and secret power more intensely played out than in lyric poetry. This is one of Keats's great themes: to suggest that beauty subverts the mind is not to suggest that its appeal is fundamentally or exclusively to the senses. It speaks to some abiding longing: for the pure, for the apparently whole. Song directed "not to the sensual ear"—in its presence, the suspicious reader is both helpless and exalted (not, I would say, cerebral responses). In such moments, the poem seems not a relic but an absolute. Time, narrative time, is abolished. The only close parallel is falling in love:

> The late cranes throwing
> their necks to the wind stay
> somewhere between
> the place that rain begins
> and the place that it ends
> they seem to exist just there
> above the horizon at least
> I only see them that way
> tossed up
> against the gray October
> light not heavy enough
> for feet to be useful or
> useless enough to make
> gravity untie its string. I'm sick
> of this stubbornness

but the earthworms
seem to think it all right
they move forward
and let the world pass
through them they eat
and eat at it, content to connect
everything through
the individual links
of their purple bodies to stay
one place would be death.
But somewhere between
the crane and the worm
between the days I pass through
and the days that pass
through me
is the mind. And memory
which outruns the body and
grief which arrests it.

—"STATUARY"

How vulnerable it seems, this poem, how fragile: a narrow
column of awareness, its movement too perpetual or too transfixed to seem headlong, despite its unpunctuated urgencies. The
elemental grandeur of the oppositions—birth and death, heaven
and earth, crane and worm—and of the mimetic structure, the
explicit lesson that "to stay / one place would be death": these
could veer close to parody or sentimentality were it not for Katherine Larson's grace and simplicity, her eerie purity of tone.
"Statuary" (like most of the poems in *Radial Symmetry*) moves
toward synthesis and repose (rather than toward ecstatic disintegration), toward containment as opposed to release. But containment and repose do not imply, here, a placid summary or

moral. Larson's repose is also a quivering suspension, in which multiple perceptions, multiple elements, are held in extended and mysterious relation. The shape is classic; in "Statuary" Larson has not so much made something new as she has given form to ancient knowledge.

This is a poem of great beauty. But beauty is also Larson's subject. So much of earth is here, at once utterly natural and wholly illumined: a grave passivity infuses this collection; experience is less sought than received. The poet is a kind of dazed Miranda, so new to the world that its every ordinariness seems an emblem of wonder. "Either everything's sublime or nothing is," she writes, and, for the span of the book, everything is.

Larson trained as a biologist, but these poems do not seem (at least to a layman) a scientist's work. They prize sensation over analytic scrutiny, the individual example over the category. Her education in science manifests here as a passion for detail (as well as a richness of reference): "I know I'm still alive because I love / to eat," she says, and everywhere in this work is the sensualist's grateful and specific avidity. The longest poem in the book, "Ghost Nets," makes a kind of dreamlike diary of being; the precision and variety of Larson's impressions, their layered abundance, correspond to the gleanings of some very lucky (and actual) nets. The implications of the title also make of the poem a protest: an informed defense of unprotected life in the face of casually pervasive human destructiveness. Each section seems a gift, an instance of harmoniousness between consciousness and flesh, the scientist's fastidious attention to detail suffused with an unexpected gentleness or solicitude toward matter:

> *Yellow snapper, bright as egg yolk.* I look at the sea and eat
> my toast.

RADIAL SYMMETRY / KATHERINE LARSON

Yesterday's lesson—the *jabonero de Cortés* or Cortez soapfish
when agitated
secretes a mucus that lathers like soap—

—"ghost nets (i)"

And this:

"Not perfection," the sea hisses, "but
originality." The innards
of a blue-eyed scallop scraped onto a plastic Safeway bag.
Soul and meat—

—"ghost nets (v)"

And this:

Every day, it happens like this.
We emerge from the pale nets of sleep like ghost shrimp
in the estuaries—
The brain humming its electric language.

Touching something in a state of becoming.

—"ghost nets (vii)"

And this:

I remember Agassiz and the sunfish. The dream in which each
breath is a perfect sphere, in which the only explanation is

pink and
voltaic—

life! Sealed inside itself like barnacles at high tide.

. . .

Down the road, large piles of murex shells—
their insides like the insides of ears.

—"GHOST NETS" (VIII)

Sequence and consequence, the drama of unfolding story, play almost no role here. Nor is data organized into argument. Rather, events and images are held together in some fluid medium that preserves them without changing them: the whole sequence has the fascination of a prism. Or perhaps the spectacle of a cell under a microscope with its unfolding revelations.

Intense sensation—I suppose the accurate word is *pleasure*—is not subjected to overt judgment or intervention. But the book as a whole is far less celebratory, less contented, than this description suggests. Larson's passion for detail carries with it, for poet as well as reader, awareness of the transience of matter, so these luminous poems give off an atmosphere of foreboding: darkness is omnipresent, encroaching.

This is especially pronounced in the love poems; erotic ravenousness is mirrored in the rapacious greed of the spirits: ". . . everywhere the spirits are hungry," she writes:

Say you leave a crust of bread on your plate.
A hundred of them could last for weeks on this.

If you said a prayer with your meal,
the offering might feed a multitude.
But then the sea always asks for more.

The speaker remembers the evening, dinner with her lover:

Sawdust floors. A mussel split and rusty
against the polished ebony of the bowl,

its sea smell like the beach at low tide . . .

And later:

She is suddenly aware of her desire for him

across the table, next to him on the bus.
But it makes her shiver, the way
those shells split apart—like half-black

moons that gave off no light, only
shadows. And they were legion.

—"LOW TIDE EVENING"

Excerpts cannot give a sense of the power such lines have in a poem that has taken its time accruing. Pacing is essential: the gravity of these unequivocal, summarizing assertions depends absolutely on the sustained images and vignettes that precede them. Statement, as it works here, has the force of inescapable truth. The last section of the four-part "Love at Thirty-two Degrees" is an example, particularly stunning in its succinctness. Here, in part, is the section preceding:

Then, there is the astronomer's wife
ascending stairs to her bed.

The astronomer gazes out,
one eye at a time,

to a sky that expands
even as it falls apart

like a paper boat dissolving in bilge.

. . .

The snow outside

is white and quiet
as a woman's slip

against cracked floorboards.
So he walks to the house

inflamed by moonlight, and slips
into the bed with his wife

her hair and arms all
in disarray

like fish confused by waves.

The final section follows:

Science—

beyond pheromones, hormones, aesthetics of bone,
every time I make love for love's sake alone,

I betray you.

This is a collection notable for its variety: formal, tonal, and—strikingly—environmental. It occurred to me that most poets who are, like Katherine Larson, deeply attuned to the natural world tend to be specifically attuned to a particular landscape. *Radial Symmetry* has no one context; its shifting backgrounds take the place of motion, giving the collection a feeling of progression or drama, as though movement in space substituted for movement in time. The effect suggests the old Hollywood mechanics of action: the driver and the passenger in the stationary car while the background lurches wildly forward and the wind machine blows apace. In a collection of poems remarkable for the stillness of the individual lyrics, such variety of setting suggests the conveyor belt, a relentless momentum alluding to the brevity or insufficiency of human life.

The overall dreamlike ambiance of this work is vividly interrupted, here and there, by poems rooted in literal (or brilliantly invented) dreams—on display in such poems is a pointed and seductive wit:

> In the dream, I am given a monkey heart
> and told to be careful how I love
> because of the resulting infection.

And later:

> A voice says, *Metamorphosis*
> *will make you ugly*. . . .

We find ourselves, soon enough, "On the lawn of my childhood house, / an operating table, doctors, / a patient under a sheet. . . ." When the sheet is lifted:

> It isn't my mother. It's the monkey.
> I bend my ear to its dying lips
> and it says: *You haven't much time—*
> *risk it all.*

—"RISK"

Wise monkey. There are other dreams, one, notably, involving Baudelaire and Margaret Mead.

But ultimately, I think, a reader will remember these poems for their beauty, the profound sense of being in the present that their sensuality embodies, and a sense, too, of its cost.

Poetry survives because it haunts and it haunts because it is simultaneously utterly clear and deeply mysterious; because it cannot be entirely accounted for, it cannot be exhausted. The poems in *Radial Symmetry* are comparatively direct, accessible, easy to read. But Katherine Larson has that gift Yeats had, what Keats had, a power to enthrall the ear, and the ear is stubborn, easily as stubborn as the mind: it will not let this voice go:

> The Milky Way sways its back
> across all of wind-eaten America
> like a dusty saddle tossed
> over your sable, lunatic horse.
> All the plains are dark.
> All the stars are cowards:
> they lie to us about their time of death
> and do nothing but dangle
> like a huge chandelier
> over nights when our mangled sobs
> make the dead reach for their guns.
> I must be one of the only girls
> who still dreams in green gingham, sees snow
> as a *steel pail's falling of frozen nails*
> like you said through pipe smoke
> on the cabin porch one night. Dear one,
> there are no nails more cold
> than those that fix you
> underground. I thought I saw you

in the moon of the auditorium
after my high school dance.
Without you, it's still hard to dance.
It's even hard to dream.

—"BROKE THE LUNATIC HORSE"

2011

FOUR

for action, for any show of effort. Damage occurred without my apparent agency and perpetuated itself indefinitely: to need to wound or—as in the books I read—murder the enemy was to display the insufficiency of self, just as action proved the existence of hurt. My idea of revenge was to prove that I had not been hurt, or had somehow exacted hurt, which (as my fantasies repeatedly demonstrated) I had miraculously transformed into something intensely to be envied. My dream was to create envy: my idea of revenge depended on the object's remaining conscious and fully aware.

Mainly, I thought about the poems I would write. In my imagination, these poems would be of a greatness that compelled, in throngs of readers, a uniform amazement, the only disagreements arising out of attempts to describe this greatness or account for it. At some point, I became aware that such response had never, in the history of literature, occurred. But I continued to feel it would occur, it had to occur, because my own response to the literature I revered was so intense, so absolute. I was in such moments suffused with awe, which seemed to me utterly different from opinion (the latter garrulous, the former dumbstruck). I felt myself in the presence of an incontestable truth or universal law. Curiously, I was not annihilated by this awe, as I expected the enemies in my fantasies to be. In them, awe would combine with feelings of horrified shame, an awareness of wrongs that could never be made right, a sense of their own lacks and misjudgments. My revenge fantasies equipped my adversaries with sophisticated and discerning literary taste; they punished themselves while I simply and transcendently existed.

This scenario was always to some degree present in my imaginative life. It became my immediate response to all public and private failure, to scorn, to betrayal, but also to much smaller events and embarrassments to which such fantasies were wildly disproportionate. But they were not simply balm. They were also fuel. They fed an existing desire to write poetry, transforming that desire into urgent ambition. They could not replace inspiration, or bribe it into existence, but they augmented inspiration with a driving sense of purpose or necessity; they animated me when I might easily have been paralyzed. It was for many years intensely pleasurable to anticipate the leisurely unfolding, over time, of revenge, with its just and glorious reversals of existing judgments and power relations.

Crucial to these fantasies was a premise of spacious or expansive time, in which the distance from the humiliated present self to the triumphant innate self could be bridged. The language of revenge depends wholly on the future tense: they'll see, they'll be sorry, and so on. Because time always seemed to me imperiled or in short supply, I did not expect age to influence what, in my fantasy life, must have been a theoretical attitude. And yet something has changed. The fantasies have vanished, and with them the tremendous surges of energy and stamina.

Something about actually attaining those ages at which, in every possible sense, time is likely to be short (or certainly rapidly diminishing) seems different from feeling constantly that one would be cut off unfairly or prematurely. In addition to that sense of expansive time, my fantasies required that my adversaries remain immutable, stable, frozen in my infinite future: the person soon to be devastated by my virtuosity and spiritual depth must be identical to the person who held an object about to be thrown at me. But my rivals and judges, like my friends and colleagues, have all been chastened and battered by time. Pity and fellow feeling have weakened vengefulness, or replaced it with a sense of collective, as opposed to hierarchical, experience, substituting an unexpected mildness and generosity for my earlier sternness and violence. These shifts have made the fixation on new targets a far less vigorous act—briefly rancorous but capable of generating no real energy.

I sometimes miss them, those immutable enemies and the power they conferred, as well as the myth of generous time on which the little raft of self seemed likely to be supported for many decades. But my fascination now with this subject is more pragmatic and anxious: how to supply those energies that were, all my life, fed by the passion for revenge.

2013

ESTRANGEMENT

In certain cases, real deprivation occurs while a parent is alive. The permanent deprivation conferred by death may seem then a liberation: it is the late-arriving explanation of or justification for absence. By extension, in providing a cause for what has long been lacked, it releases the child from a sense of culpability. Finally the outside matches the inside. The family, finally, is not whole. No one can say otherwise.

It seems to me that the child who grows up in a family of this kind feels acutely a sense of secrecy: the truth is not available. Signals that truth is not to be demanded, nor established deceits queried, give rise to feelings of extreme precariousness or danger. In fact, there may be no dramatic secret at all. There may simply be embarrassment, the long-standing social habit of substituting fiction for candor. Regardless, the child feels that something that could destroy the family is being withheld. Ultimately, the child wishes it to be withheld because he wishes not to be destroyed. But he also wishes to know, resents the obligation to participate in a fraud. Whether the absent parent is physically present or not, the absence has not been convincingly accounted for or acknowledged. In either case, the child learns quickly because his motivation is deep: if needs will not be met, best to be self-sustaining. He learns to act a part, as do all family members in this system. For convenience, he disguises himself as a child as later he may disguise himself as a lover or scholar or family man. In any case, the integrity of the family Christmas card will have been preserved.

I mean here to distinguish absence from death, in that the missing parent continues to exist in time, so the tormenting hope of reunion remains plausible. The predicament of the child, in a period that may be prolonged by the continuation of the theoretically intact family, creates attitudes and dilemmas eerily resembling characteristics that have emerged in American poetry in the last quarter century.

The ancient and, to poetry, rewarding subject of loss has gradually given way: cataclysmic disappearance has been replaced by perpetual absence, an event replaced by a mood. In a world from which extremes of feeling have been banished, the distinction between dramatic loss and everyday experience is blurred or diminished. There will be no such shock again. Loss is the routine condition now, the overcast day, not the eclipse or storm. And a wholesome distaste for sentiment has calcified into a brittle amalgam of suspicion and wit.

Dan Chiasson's father never materialized, though things were known about him, principally that he was still alive. And yet Chiasson's poems inhabit anxieties of the kind I have described; he is obsessed with childhood, specifically a child's negotiations with a reality that does not, somehow, match the reality he is told he lives in. He sees, more deeply than most, the solitude of childhood, preserved in the strange universe of the adult world, with its codes and signs and signals:

. . . bear with me while I try to convey what I want to convey
my father's distance and yet the tendency of distant things
to become central; my tidelike ups and downs, up-downs
and down-ups and the influence of a superstellar body
upon me; my "poetry" as I hazard to call these writings;
bear with me because this movie, though vividly a record
of somebody saying something, has no sound of its own,
which means I might as well not have a mouth . . .

And later in this long poem, the title poem of *Where's the Moon,
There's the Moon*, in which a child is reading, or looking at, a book:

In our inattention, the child has come close to finishing
The Moonkeeper's Son, and has learned how a grown man
    yearns
to go back to his time, beside his father, on the moon,
and dreams he is back there in childhood, which is
a kind of moon (this point the author intends), though mine
had a lot more pewter figurines of Christ strewn around it
than the moon, at least as it is classically represented,
would; a kind of moon, and fathers come and go, don't
    they . . .

Dan Chiasson is a poet of dazzling intellectual resources and
unmatched sophistication. His temperament is rapacious, wily;
his ear quick; his range of reference memorable, in part for the
casual ease of its uses. And yet the poems are more profound,
more original, than their coolly enigmatic surfaces suggest.
These surfaces seem a kind of dare or taunt to the reader, who
is meant to sense, beneath Chiasson's ruses and diversions, the
immutable loss and sorrow and fear that give rise to them. The
alertness here is the alertness of flight: all Chiasson's worldliness,

all his control, lay bare the constant dread beneath the surface, as though inventiveness and quickness could fend off catastrophe, or protect the precarious truce that has been made with reality.

This is a self in hiding or disguised, its evasions and flights impossible to track because they are not here-to-there escapes but rather a commitment to ceaseless mobility or a very specific and very revealing form of hiding, ventriloquism. Chiasson has inhabited, at various times, an elephant, a mosaic of a hare, a thread, the eye of a needle, and a revolving door, this last providing a pithy analysis of family or social life with its impossible-to-decode rules and signs:

> I spit and swallow with equal gusto.
> Spitting is not a sign of disgust.
> Swallowing is not a sign of hunger.
>
> Casting out is not a sign of anger.
> Allowing in is not affection.
> I chug along, doing what I'm meant to.

No disguise is more effective than compliance, no flight more devious than the route of the revolving door.

Chiasson's obsessions have not shifted. And yet each book marks a deepening, discovers some new tone or structure that allows the present to incorporate the past more subtly, without falsifying it in any way.

His powers were not immediately apparent. *The Afterlife of Objects* documents technical and intellectual virtuosity. It seemed to me, when I read it in light of what followed, comparable to the school figures or compulsory figures in the Olympic skating competition, an event television viewers do not see. In fact, we probably wouldn't know a perfect circle from a flawed circle, though we are reminded by the commentary that the great expressive skaters are not invariably perfect technicians. So, too, in other arts. But the conjoining of expressive capacity with brilliant technique—in dance, think of Farrell or Baryshnikov—produces an art of thrilling variety and daring.

Dan Chiasson seemed at first essentially a master of style: armored, elusive, fundamentally mistrustful, after the current fashion. What has come to distinguish him from others is his insight into the idiom of the time, in which nostalgia and irony replace overt intensity. Chiasson is uniquely a poet for whom hiddenness is a profound psychic truth, a poet for whom guardedness corresponds to rather than precludes inwardness. The authentic self is performed as a false self, but every pose is a clue. Hiddenness and flight are not devices by which interiority is fended off. They are maps to insight and every detail of performance is a glimpse of the obsessed self.

As book has succeeded book, Chiasson's poems have made these performances increasingly resonant and poignant, the structures more and more supple and capacious, in their elegance capable of bearing unimaginable weight. Fictions, inventions, plays, masquerades: these are still central. The poems continue to rely on and exploit artifice, but this, after all, is how a child tells his story. Which, in *Bicentennial*, is the story of how a child (himself) is provided with a father (himself).

Midway through the title poem, a young nun takes out a coin from the collection she has brought to the convent, a ". . . Standing Liberty quarter / Engraved with the first initial of a boy / She'd dated, and who'd taken her to the fair." This is the climax, for the speaker, of the interlude:

I had the distinct impression she still loved him,
The way the whole afternoon led up
To her getting the quarter from her drawer,

And putting it on the TV tray
Next to her bed, next to the rosary,
And watched me react when she said
The word *boy*. . . .

The boy standing there—the speaker—is a collector, too, and knows the value of every coin; he wonders "How much less it now was worth engraved":

Now she puts the coin into the drawer, and
We move inside my mind to the Paris skyline,
Where an enormous Ferris wheel appears,
Lit by the light it generates, a wheel
That spins and spins nowhere, nowhere,
All night, whether we watch it or not,
And children are having their childhoods right now,
This late in time, as though they had to stand in line

Just to be born . . .

There is a section break after the line, so the Ferris wheel, which has given its name and essence to an earlier poem, stays a bit in the mind, an emblem of detachment and escape—but this is a new kind of escape, endless, without destination, an image of being carried or borne. The children standing in the line are waiting, the poem tells us,

Just to be born, get on, and ride, and
From the top they see the sliver of history

Fate is allowing them to see, before
They disembark and scatter, some to joy,
Some to misery, and whether they live
For a hundred years or die, as some have,
Tomorrow, this is the childhood these children
Are having, which is something I remind

My own children, all the time—I say,
You are having your childhood now;
And they say, yes, Daddy, and I say,
Jokingly, but not really, how do you feel it is going,
And they light up and say, Great,
Which is just what I would have said as a kid
If someone—though who would it have been?—
Had asked me this very same question:

The Ferris wheel is the revolving door from *Where's the
Moon, There's the Moon* turned vertical, celestial, a circle like the
sullied quarter (worth both less and more). In "Bicentennial,"
though, repetition allows for mutation or correction. This father
speaks to his children as though that long-absent father had finally
appeared, filled with all the information and wisdom it had been
his part to convey; he speaks to his children as to reasoning beings, the joking question also a reminder to stay conscious.
What follows has the sweetness of a book for new readers: the
generous-hearted children may not understand the question but
they know the answer. The children reassure their father, who
has appealed, after all, to their analytic capacities at a moment
when the script can still be modified. Their father needs to
know that his moodiness and withdrawals have not crippled the
children or destroyed their childhoods—that period in which
trust in the world is still possible. The children's collaboration

contains, it seems, no fear or anxiety, only solicitous tenderness, a mirror of their father's feelings toward them. The question changes the narrative slightly (no one has actually asked it before), and the response the poet would like to have made is now the response of his children. Possibly not the truth, but spoken out of a fullness of heart nevertheless.

The Ferris wheel they have all ridden together is also the Ferris wheel of a miraculous "play," very formal and very short, about adult passion and adult regret. The cast is small: a Man and a Faerie. The Faerie (playing her guitar) tells the Man:

> Your symbol is the Ferris wheel, which gobbles
> Its own tail, the peaceful circle,
>
> The serene return to origin and out again,
> As though the return never happened,
>
> The journey undoing the return,
> The return undoing the journey,
>
> The pattern made from the pattern it traces:
> A pattern that, by tracing it, it erases.

The man remembers his children's loving the Ferris wheel in Paris:

> . . . I can remember thinking,
> How odd that I am thinking,
> Not about the Paris skyline
>
> (Which I had never seen, though I was thirty-nine)
> But about the Paris Ferris wheel,
> Not at all interested in the Champs, or Notre Dame,

It felt like an affirmation of what is really human.
I thought of community theater for some reason.
I had a deep wish that someday

My boys would play
Clara in a drag version of *The Nutcracker*,
The weird things people do to make each other happy—

Before long, the ride ends. The Faerie begins to weep uncontrollably. We realize—we are told—that the two have been,
in the past, lovers. And the man wishes they could perform
the play over (toward, we infer, a less wrenching end). We are
instructed to think of the poem as a play, the lines repeated
nightly, the Faerie's tears shed nightly—many men, centuries of
men, and many Faeries, all imprisoned in the same narrative, the
Ferris wheel corresponding to the immutable storyline.

Bicentennial is, in a sense, a meditation on circles; the Ferris
wheel is, I think, the circle's most profound iteration. The calm
progress of the wheel is both escape from earth and, as well, a
means by which perspective is shifted. Time seems, for the
period of the ride, more like eternity and less like what the line
(to invoke a competing geometric term) represents as it sprints
from birth to death but never back. In this extraordinary book,
the line and circle coexist. Nothing is just one thing: the coin
tainted by attachment is also the coin the young nun values, different from all other Standing Liberty quarters. And the realistic
boy, who hasn't as yet felt these emotions, feels a kind of awe in
their presence as well as mild contempt.

Biographical fact shapes human life, but it does not predict
the imaginative constructions that given materials may produce.
Dan Chiasson's gift could have elaborated itself in endless dex-
terities; human attachment has made this art not only adroit but

passionate and worried and exposed. The births of his own children have allowed the recasting of a pivotal role; the absent father can, at last, be replaced. The children in these poems can have two real parents. They can be encouraged to think about their experiences, to discuss them. There can be a home for the wit and plangency that are the poems' signature. It is a fantasy, of course—as it is a curiosity that Chiasson's real father *does* die, his remoteness becoming complete, final.

Nothing in that past can be changed or restored. But the present can change the way it is thought about. In this new enactment, presence can replace absence, which is the best that can be managed in human time.

2016

FEAR OF HAPPINESS

Among the distinguishing characteristics of mythic or totemic stories, let me call two of the most obvious to your attention: first, by definition, they stay in the mind—durability distinguishes the archetypal from the anecdotal. Second, more peculiarly, they mutate, or our perceptions of their fundamental truths change. Perhaps "mutate" is inaccurate; better to say that what magnetizes attention shifts. A story with staying power will offer a variety of possible centers of focus (though these may be perceived sequentially rather than simultaneously). Stories of this type, whatever their scale (and they may, superficially, resemble the anecdote), possess a certain interior spaciousness within clear outlines, so that they seem, on reflection, at once copious and eternally unresolved. In simpler terms, every time I see *Children of Paradise* it has a different hero. And every time I read *Wuthering Heights*, I feel a different moral or emotional imperative. When I was sixteen: value passion. Meaning sacrifice anything to it. When I was twenty-five: be wary of passion's tendency to screen narcissism. And so on.

All this holds true, as well, in the realm of the personal. We have, each of us, certain charged stories or referents, the sorts of stories we tell those people we wish to befriend, so that they will see what has formed us. What is odd is that, over time, the same story can be used to make different points, though we may continue to befriend the same sorts of attractive strangers.

When I was in my early twenties and beginning, finally, to master in psychoanalysis the range of symptoms I had been controlled by, when I was able to perform dazzling acts like eating in the presence of other human beings; when I no longer needed to do the same tasks daily in the same order; when I was no longer wholly withdrawn (which is the common legacy of shame), I found myself suddenly terrified. A vision of desolate normalcy presented itself. I was terrified, specifically, that normalcy—whatever I meant by that—would somehow eradicate the need for, or capacity for, what even then I ceremoniously called my work. For five years I had been struggling desperately to become whole and sane in order to rejoin a world made, as I saw it, entirely of the whole and the sane, a world free of the humiliating loneliness and fear that constituted my reality. And I remember very clearly my panic and the terms in which I accused my analyst, who had conspired in all this: he was going to make me so happy I wouldn't write. I also remember his response. He looked at me directly, an event in itself rare (and possibly the underlying reason I remember this exchange). His response was memorably succinct. The world, he told me, will provide you sorrow enough.

For the egoist, a revolutionary concept. What interested me in this story initially was the analyst's unprecedented directness together with the sense that his personal history had, briefly, entered the room. Also the strange unease his response provoked. My confidence in him was, for complex reasons, shaken. He had no right to be so present in the room, to substitute for Delphic silence and sly direction a remark so tainted by the personal. Also, I thought he was wrong. That is, I thought the world couldn't possibly provide as much anguish as I needed. If he was wrong, I had duped him; if I had duped him, he was no longer reliable. Did he really know how wily I was, how inherently powerful (despite present restrictions of performance); did he really think the world was any match for such force? *I* generated my sorrow; nothing and no one could be trusted to meet my fierce and specific standard. Later, his remark took on an aspect of prophecy, which always has about it something of the echo— in this case, what was echoed was my own early perception of the world in exactly the aspect my analyst noted. Growing up, I had transformed myself into the agent of the inescapable; I couldn't bear chance, as a principle; I saw the world as whimsical and lethal, a machine for doing harm. And I took over its work, to avoid being its victim.

In fact, it wasn't until very recently that I began to read this exchange from another angle, to examine a certain underlying assumption. Specifically, why was I so sure unhappiness was essential to the making of art? Or, more precisely, what attributes of what I imagined happiness to be did I believe subverted creation? Plainly, I ascribed to happiness some opacity or chronic unresponsiveness; accurately enough, I saw responsiveness as essential to the creative act, but my definition seemed to limit it to a particular type. I saw responsiveness, it appears, as resulting from a keenly felt abrasiveness between the self and the world, as though that boundary could be perceived only in the most dramatic and negative terms. What is emphasized in such definitions is the self, not as a secure pole or referent, but as a fundamental dimness clarified by oppositions. Its very haziness gives rise to its avidity; it strives constantly to define itself (as more clearly realized selves do not), and it is able to define itself only relative to what it is not.

In the period of which I've been speaking, whatever my surprise at my analyst's observation, I had a somewhat diminished stake in maintaining the presumably fecund misery from which, in my view, he insisted on rescuing me. Luckily, or so I presently believe, I was protected from my asserted wish to shore up suffering, to stabilize it, by the intensity of my suffering at that time. I had, too, this recent memory: I began analysis imperiled not by happiness but by despair; in the years when that was most acute, I was wholly silent, on the page and in the world.

Set aside, for the moment, natural speculation regarding the talent of the artist, of the restless, demanding, insatiable soul, for actually attracting and sustaining serenity. Assume, for the moment, that some parenthesis of well-being does, from time to time, open, even in the lives of people of this type. Think, for now, only of the meticulous resistance to that state, which perhaps some of you have felt already. As in the moment when love ceases to be narrative, ceases to be dramatic capitulation, and the single next thing appears to be sterility, a vista of suburbs. As though the suburbs, as though the mutations of love in time, could only be sterile.

Curiously, once the question is posed, once the whole issue of the relation of unhappiness to the making of art comes under scrutiny, the sources of this connection grow clear. They derive, I think, from the original set of impulses and rewards that draw individual minds to this vocation. Most artists, most writers certainly, are drawn to the creative act by its capacity to promote catharsis and, through catharsis, affirm a faltering sense of power. Pre-existing anguish, in being given form, is externalized; in being externalized, it is transformed. Transformed, as opposed to neutralized: it gives rise to its extreme opposite. What results, for the artist or nascent artist, is euphoria. Not only are anxiety and tension temporarily relieved—something comes into being to which the self bonds with a kind of desperate ardor. Unfortunately, the learned dynamics of catharsis, the conversion via writing of despair to elation, will not sustain a creative gift any more than the animating rages of youth can be mechanically prolonged. Equally unfortunately, the more efficiently catharsis reins in suffering, and the headier the sense of elation that results from the making of a work of art, the greater the self's investment in art. In art, obviously, but also in the increasingly ritualized process leading to art. And ultimately an odd shadow of dependency or addiction creeps in. Suffering gradually becomes the presumed first condition of elation or triumph; the more efficiently catharsis works, the more likely it is that an artist is being created, a person, that is, whose sense of power and worth depends primarily on these surrogates, these objects that have been created.

This dependency is my subject, and, beyond it, a certain practical speculation as to the usefulness, to an artist, of happiness, in whatever form it may happen to present itself. By which term I mean not euphoria (which is in any case familiar to people of this type, a state of grace like falling in love, and, like falling in love, an intoxication)—not euphoria, but that strange country I glimpsed in my analyst's office, happiness defined as well-being.

The artist, that person whose sense of self absolutely depends on continued creation, begins to connect his survival as a powerful or, in any case, viable being to despair; despair, however damaging, however threatening, however eroding of the physical self, cannot damage what is perceived as being truly essential: the ability to make art. Quite the reverse: this it preserves and sustains. The real threat, according to this reasoning, is happiness which, by removing active unrest, sabotages creative life, which proceeds from an accumulated misery that demands cathartic release. The dependency on dissatisfaction, the courting of it by the artist—this is less a Faustian compact than a destructive, or at least limiting, hope. Destructive not in the obvious sense, in that it places at risk or undermines the whole world of relationship, or physical soundness, or social function, but destructive in exactly those terms by which the self experiences its deepest sense of authentic being: what is threatened with destruction in this system is the artist, who was born, long before, not only of will but of its hopeless and powerless opposite, out of lack of control.

At the heart of this dilemma, the tacit rejection of happiness, is the problem of control, which is, first, the problem of vulnerability. It is the latter that attaches to happiness, to any form of *having.* Like material wealth, emotional or spiritual wealth stands to be lost: better the security of having nothing than the anxiety of well-being, which can only diminish. Moreover, the willed renunciation of well-being acts as a kind of protection: no one, the artist reasons, gets everything. So renunciation of what others hold most dear shores up, in the artist, what *he* holds most dear, his talent. And whatever its size, it is likely to be perceived, with some regularity, as precarious. The unfamiliar unnerves; in this system, misery and despair tend to produce an odd response— they are at least known; they generate no obsession with subtraction, since they are that state to which subtraction ultimately descends. When nothing exists that can be taken away, a secret power asserts itself, a sense of control that well-being systematically threatens or erodes.

An early form of the pattern will seem, I believe, familiar. Put simply: once the addiction is established, despair becomes safety, and the artist begins to attempt to control or limit the ways in which he is influenced, trying to replicate indefinitely those circumstances or states of mind believed to be favorable to the making of art. This puts the matter, perhaps, too optimistically, makes choice seem to exist. Whereas the artist is, more likely, a being who has found a marginally viable existence that he or she goes on to frantically defend. This frenzy is natural, a function of the conviction that the alternative to present modes is not different modes but nothing, the abyss. The cleaving to pattern can coexist with apparently expansive or experimental behaviors, since what is being cleaved to is an edge, that is, precariousness. Only those experiences or behaviors characteristic of what we can loosely call normalcy or serenity are ruled out. And this comes to be a ruling against the unknown in its most radical form, a ruling made, oddly enough, in the name of risk.

Over time, the true danger, the true sabotaging domestic space, becomes that edge to which panic roots the creative being. The words by which this edge is described affirm its glamorous shakiness; in fact, it has become wholly conservative space. I have seen this particular timidity in my own nature; I have watched it and heard it in my students. It fuels those questions about the future in which multiple desires or leanings figure: Is it dangerous for a writer to be an academic? Will medicine (or law or business) destroy my gift? And, particularly among women: Should I marry? Should I have children? And although no one can guarantee that the married doctor with children will also write enduring poetry, or that the passionate adolescent who finally permits himself maturity and pleasure will evolve into a deeper thinker, the person who, through cautious clinging to the known, the ostensibly safe, arrests or constrains his native fascination with medicine or desire for family is diminishing the possibility of his making original art. Meaning art unique to a specific and profoundly lived experience. Only such art attains the force and durability of paradigm. Whereas the "paradigmatic" artistic life, the edge I have been describing, when clung to through will, yields up an art hardly deserving of that name, an art too predictable in its judgments and, finally, too superficial to attract attention over time.

Behind the choice of despair (as opposed to the accident of despair, as opposed, also, to the tragic vision, which is another matter)—behind this choice is the unarticulated assumption that the life most conducive to art is entirely empty of anything interesting enough to distract from writing or satisfying enough to replace the need to write. But the earlier, the formative despair, the galvanizing memorable despair of adolescence, is not replicated through willful perpetuations and imitations. And the sadder form of these questions about the future is not question but statement, the asserted decision to turn from a natural bent lest the gift be damaged.

This is the mathematics of insurance (which insulates against the more painful perception of injustice). The need to write, or make art, gives rise to the wish to keep alive and affirm *only* the creative being and suppress or constrain all satellite selves. And as the only emotion held to be entirely safe to that being is unhappiness, the only congenial conditions turmoil and retreat, the only activity held to be free of environmental contamination and harmful distraction is the reading of great literature.

But once literature is sought for these reasons, it changes. Whatever it was once, infinite and necessary air, it now becomes restriction, less that air than the conditioned air of a sealed room. That is, it is being valued for what it is not; it is being used to screen out impurity. Or, to use another figure, it becomes something like steamed vegetables, safe because they contain nothing known to cause harm. To read for these reasons, to read to stay safe, is to undermine the essential capacity and service of literature. Those gifts become accessible again when less elevated pleasures are accommodated. Pleasures like cooking and bad movies, pleasures like the indefensible television's. I believe these pleasures also nourish though in mysterious ways: they relax the soul. They are the little worlds in which the spirit is not tested. The difficulty is that the artist cannot take pride in what they nourish because pride, in him, is so utterly connected to the creative act, and because his imagination concerning that act is limited by fear to a kind of magical system, rife with taboos and forbidden gestures. And, to people of this type, what is not a source of pride is, de facto, a source of shame.

Let me urge now the utility of happiness. First: understand that happiness or well-being does not automatically produce a poetry or prose that sounds these same sanguine notes. What is far more likely, certainly in the artist whose vision is tragic, is that some measure of well-being strengthens him sufficiently to enable the deepest excavations. The spirit, fortified, can afford to go more profoundly, more resourcefully, into its materials, being less imperiled. But principally I wish to argue for well-being as a means of increasing openness to diversity and, by extension, as a means by which the artist increases his range or, possibly, locates a fundamental subject. Dependency on despair acts to limit the subjects with which the mind contends or engages to those subjects available at the time the rituals of catharsis were discovered. In my own experience, periods of despair resemble one another, even in the sense that each seems, at the moment and despite antecedents, the true platonic desolation, the terminus, the authentic nadir. Whereas happiness surprises in both its advent and its causes: it releases information. What unhappiness tends to perpetuate is an isolating and, usually, limiting fixation on the self; except in the very rarest cases, this is bound to be an aesthetic limitation. Whereas well-being, in paying homage to its sources and causes, seeks out the world, a place likely to be more varied than the self, particularly than the artist self, so long protected from dubious influence. In periods of well-being, the worlds of external object and event enter perception. Focus moves outward as well as inward.

I believe my analyst was correct in his remark. The world, whether zealously monitored or allowed a looser hand—the world will indeed provide sorrow enough. The intensity and frequency and type of that sorrow depend to a painful extent on luck, which is called luck because it cannot be controlled or lured or annexed. We can't do anything about whatever luck decides to do with us. We can, however, refuse the narrowness of that determined unhappiness the will insists on. Occasionally something will give pleasure, will actually charm or divert or entertain, will, to use that terrifying word, disarm. Insofar as our fearful, compulsive, rigid natures allow, I think we should welcome what follows.

1990

PERMISSIONS ACKNOWLEDGMENTS

The following essays appeared in earlier forms in other publications:

"American Originality" (*The Threepenny Review*, Fall 2001)
"American Narcissism" (*The Threepenny Review*, Winter 1998)
"Ersatz Thought" (*The Threepenny Review*, Winter 1999)
"On *Buddenbrooks*" (*The Threepenny Review*, Summer 2003)
"Story Tellers" (*American Poetry Review*, July/August 1997, vol. 26, issue 4)
"On Realism" (*The Threepenny Review*, Summer 2004)
"The Culture of Healing" (presented at a symposium at the Boston Institute for Psychotherapy)
"On Revenge" (*The Threepenny Review*, Fall 2013)
"Estrangement" (*The Threepenny Review*, Summer 2016)
"Fear of Happiness" (Hopwood Lecture, University of Michigan, 1996; *Michigan Quarterly Review*, 1996)

Grateful acknowledgment is made to Yale University Press for permission to reprint selections from the following books:

The Cuckoo, Peter Streckfus (2004)
Crush, Richard Siken (2005)